Take Action

Move toward the Realization of Your Dreams

(How to Win Laziness, Build Your Self-discipline Overcome Your Fears)

Philip Fedler

Published By **Jordan Levy**

Philip Fedler

All Rights Reserved

Take Action: Move toward the Realization of Your Dreams (How to Win Laziness, Build Your Self-discipline Overcome Your Fears)

ISBN 978-1-7771462-6-9

No part of this guidebook shall be reproduced in any form without permission in writing from the publisher except in the case of brief quotations embodied in critical articles or reviews.

Legal & Disclaimer

The information contained in this book is not designed to replace or take the place of any form of medicine or professional medical advice. The information in this book has been provided for educational & entertainment purposes only.

The information contained in this book has been compiled from sources deemed reliable, and it is accurate to the best of the Author's knowledge; however, the Author cannot guarantee its accuracy and validity and cannot be held liable for any errors or omissions. Changes are periodically made to this book. You must consult your doctor or get professional medical advice before using any of the suggested remedies, techniques, or information in this book.

Upon using the information contained in this book, you agree to hold harmless the Author from and against any damages, costs, and expenses, including any legal fees potentially resulting from the application of any of the information provided by this guide. This disclaimer applies to any damages or injury caused by the use and application, whether directly or indirectly, of any advice or information presented, whether for breach of contract, tort, negligence, personal injury, criminal intent, or under any other cause of action.

You agree to accept all risks of using the information presented inside this book. You need to consult a professional medical practitioner in order to ensure you are both able and healthy enough to participate in this program.

Table Of Contents

Chapter 1: You, A Dream Being 1

Chapter 2: Your Morning Affirmations Can Be Your Wings 10

Chapter 3: Leaps Of Failures To Climb 19

Chapter 4: Motivation To Inspire You 26

Chapter 5: Your Flame 41

Chapter 6: Your Circle Of Support 51

Chapter 7: Believing In Yourself 62

Chapter 8: Setting And Achieving Goals . 75

Chapter 9: Overcoming Procrastination And Self-Doubt 80

Chapter 10: The Importance Of Planning And Prioritizing 85

Chapter 11: Building Habits And Consistency 89

Chapter 12: The Role Of Positive Mindset And Attitude 94

Chapter 13: Seeking Support And Accountability 98

Chapter 14: Accepting Failure And Learning From Your Mistakes 103

Chapter 15: Living A Fulfilling Life Via Action 105

Chapter 16: Why Should You Trust This Book To Change Your Life? 111

Chapter 17: You Know You Want Better For Yourself 124

Chapter 18: What Are You Going To Do About It? 135

Chapter 19: Changing The Mindset 138

Chapter 1: You, A Dream Being

"All humans are dreamers. The act of dreaming connects all mankind." Jack Kerouac. Jack Kerouac

Do you recall those days when you were a child and people would inquire about what you'd like being as you get older? At that time it was already planning, having an idea of goals that were abstract, full of colours, as well as specifics. When you were a kid there was a perfect heart, and an endless array of possibilities. You could be whatever you wanted to become.

As you get older, your fears begin to increase and confusions become more prevalent. Sometime, you'll be wondering what happened to the fantasizing child. However, you also know that you're and will always be a person who dreams. Whatever transpires in your existence, your biggest goals are right there - dancing softly in the face of difficulties and failings.

First and foremost, identify your goal and do not fear it.

E'yen Gardner, the author of Detox 21: 21 Days of purifying the soul, said "When you begin the journey to your dream, you'll encounter apprehensions as you've never traveled like this before. While you travel and you discover there is nothing to be afraid of. By overcoming your fears, you offer those around you the hope that, if they follow their ambitions, they'll succeed in their goals."

Dreams aren't just the ones you have, but those of many others as well. Therefore, when you take ownership of your vision and are able to recognize that it's yours, it's an opportunity to affirm your own voice. It is a like the voice that is hidden by other people. If you're brave enough to share your personal goals, the universe will beat for you.

Then why do they be afraid to magnify their ambitions?

* "What ifs" bombard them as they're unsure and uncertain if they're enough

* A few of their relatives, friends and family members have urged them to stay away from them, citing practical reasons.

The possibility that something negative could occur in the process

* Perhaps not all are going to support them.

* Failure

Below are a few easy ways to get started acknowledging, magnifying and taking ownership of your dreams

1.) Recognize that you've got goals:

It is possible that you are too shy or frightened to acknowledge that you've got desires. The excuses that you think you've neglected them are just way of telling others that you've put them away. Let them go today. Be aware that you're worthwhile. Your hopes are your personal voice, your way of communicating towards the world. Find and follow. In the event that you do not follow, you're just taking your own advice.

2.) Note down your goals

In order to have the ability to visualize your desires, you need to note them down. Note them down on paper. Then, look over each one with faith. Do not judge dreams. Note them in front of others. It is recommended to write down your thoughts in a journal, whether it's a journal or an email on your phone take it up. It's an excellent opportunity to write down your goals.

3.) Divide your goals into steps

The biggest dreams begin with the smallest start. It is not necessary to start with a roaring force to pursue your goals. Develop a list of tiny steps to get there your goal/s. This makes it seem more simple. If your dreams are simpler to look like, the more eager you'll be to make your dreams come true. Be sure to think of your goals as small pieces. You can have them!

4.) Be aware of the obstacles which are preventing you from achieving your goals:

It is said that if you have the will to do it and a plan, it will be possible to achieve. If you believe you've had a hard time convincing yourself to pursue your goals Think again. Consider these points and come up with ways to address the challenges. It is only when we end our pursuits as we begin to build barriers of our own. If you spot a roadblock Be aware of how to deal with each. Don't look at the whole because it could overpower you.

5.) Meet people who be there to support your efforts:

They will provide you with confidence and strength - particularly in the toughest situations. They'll always be there to lift you on and support you throughout the process. Do not forget to express your gratitude and to acknowledge their role throughout your journey and fulfilling your ambitions. Do not label people in a way that implies shaming the other. Be amazed by the world around you inviting anyone you meet - you'll never know the magical gifts they could bring to you.

6.) Do yourself a favor and pat yourself for the accomplishments you have made:

You deserve it! One of the most enjoyable aspects of fulfilling your dream is the process. This is the element that develops your character, and it's the part will be remembered the most. You deserve a reward whenever you accomplish something or get over the obstacles to reach the goals you have set. Make yourself feel loved throughout the day. Being kind to yourself will help you develop that self-love you have always wanted.

7.) Be aware that the fear of being afraid won't go away.

There are moments when it is difficult to know if are able to realize your ambitions or if you are worthy of living the ones you want to live. The fear is an inherent part of our human condition. It is not a reason to be afraid. This should be considered an indication that you are pursuing to achieve your goals with a lot of. If you are feeling a significant feeling of anxiety, make sure to relax and do not think about the negative feelings. Allow it to fade away and direct your attention on the actions towards your goal.

For guidance in overcoming every single day, make the habit of a momentary silence and a gentle upward lift every day. The following methods:

• Find a peaceful place to sit and contemplate.

* Lay down or sit in a comfortable position.

Concentrate on breath - breathe slowly inhale and be aware of the strength of your desires within your.

Inhale deeply and experience the peace that will come from each one of them will come true.

Repeat the steps until you're completely calm and relaxed.

It's true that you're an idealist regardless of what. If you keep the dream within you and make enough time to keep it in your mind and strive for the goal, there is no limit to what you can achieve. Because it's only the moment you remember the spark that you have within yourself, and when you begin to believe that you're set for an astronomical increase.

Chapter 2: Your Morning Affirmations Can Be Your Wings

"What you do in the initial 5-10 minutes will determine your mood, energy and happiness for the remainder of your morning and all day long.

Positive affirmations begin your day off with a positive start. They equip you with the skills to deal with situations easily and ease because you've already proved that you're prepared for the challenges. Your mind is fully prepared to be successful and happy and your body follows your heart and with it you are able to conquer every day." Prolific Living

When you dream of your goals every single day, rise positive in your thoughts. It is possible that you are as active with everyone else, but do not let yourself get caught up in the moment. In a hurry, you can make you lose touch with your goals.

Suzanne Glover of Effective Positive Thinking offers, "In a nutshell, positive affirmations are the most fully absorbed by our brains the moment we get up in the early morning. Our brains are the most susceptible to thoughts because the brainwaves of our bodies shift between the sleep state of delta to the awakening condition of the alpha."

What is the Alpha state? It is the place where magic occurs. Alpha state refers to a state that is peaceful, relaxed and free of attention and stimulation. It is characterized by alpha waves at a frequency of 8 to 13 Hz as recorded by an electroencephalograph and is accompanied by feelings of tranquility and a lack of tension and anxiety

Simply put, when you start your day in a calm and relaxed way that it can sustain your peace for the remainder throughout the entire day. This can help bring clarity and allow more space to your desires.

This is an excellent routine to start your day by doing:

From the time you awake, avoid using your smartphone, or using the internet for checking emails or updates on social media.

While you're lying on your mattress, make sure you are your eyes fixed on the ceiling then begin to concentrate on the breath.

* Think of your dreams for a moment and breathe in...1...2...3...then, breathe out...1...2...3.

Repeat the process another few instances until you're calm and relaxed.

"Drift" your thoughts. As an example, "Today, I will make steps to accomplish _____. Today, I am positive about my greatest dream."

Also, you can consider it in your head at least a few times. Be aware that if you are struggling beginning, you can select a soothing music to listen to it in order to maintain your at peace. We recommend using instruments that help to achieve peace. We all know that life has been hectic and you might have difficulty adjusting or restructuring your routine.

If you repeat this routine every throughout the day, until it is the norm, it affects your mind, and your mind. Your doors in life are opened for you to be able to accept the abundance. Abundance finds us. The abundance will be found if you allow it to. Be always open. You're exactly what you've been waiting for.

Remember these wonderful words "Dare to imagine in positive ways. Make choices that benefit your family, society and worldwide society."

Many stories confirm the effectiveness of affirmations.

When you wake up, it's best to slow down. Have you ever had the time when you truly enjoyed breakfast and not having to hurry? What was the last time you took time to do a quick exercise or stretching? Have you ever had a moment when you took a sip of coffee or tea slow enough to allow you to enjoy the warmth of a cup?

Are you running late to make it to work? Are you running late to avoid the congestion? What was the last time you took time to appreciate every sight or person you encounter when you walk to work? There are many motives to rush, but right now, create a positive impact.

A slowing-down and affirming our hopes early in the day can create your life with lots of joy as well as optimism and satisfaction.

Here's a sample of many morning affirmations stories that truly will make you feel warm and fuzzy:

I've tried positive affirmations in the past, however when I hit a low moment in my personal life, I was introduced to morning affirmations. I determined to create a solid strategy and utilize them daily. In the aftermath of losing a loved one throughout my life, I was able to use only for 2 minutes per day, at the beginning of each day occasionally during the evening. This method of practice has transformed for myself. I don't know how to show how my thoughts have changed during this period. I am definitely feeling more content and positive and am more active and out as well as doing a lot more things in my day-to-day life. They've been a major lifesaver for me as I felt like my life was falling apart in my life as a result of circumstances that I believed were outside of my control. Positive affirmations are easy and may provide all the motivation you require. I recommend that everyone give these a serious trial for two weeks and notice the change. -Paul Peterson, Austin, Texas

For your convenience, here's a second short snippet of text:

My new affirmation for me was"I Love You, Steve. I am in love with you. The affirmation that I used to make transformed everything. After the first time I made it clear, I began laughing because it was so strange to declare that I loved myself. My face then changed. There was a lump within my throat.

"I love you, Steve. I love you." I choked up.

It was so hard to stand there looking me at the mirror, and hearing my voice say "I love you," which I quickly realized that I didn't think I could believe it. I began to shed tears through my eyes. What am I doing not saying the words to myself, I thought. Do I really have all my life, not ever truly being myself? As time went by this old notion faded off and I saw me as I am. Then, for the first time in my life, I was able to love and respect myself.

It was the beginning for a transformational process that started with an easy affirmation that led to acceptance of myself and eventually, the courage to share my truth regarding my sexuality to family and friends.

In the morning, dew hangs from the leaves' tips. As the sun slowly rises its head, you can are able to see the newness in everything including mountains and daily people striving to begin the process over. Start each day with a smile within your soul. This is your second chance of getting the life you want in your own hands.

Affirmations for the morning are similar to wings that could flap in the future, and let you fly. Imagine being a small bird with aspirations, then you're preparing yourself for the flight. Every morning, you are able to build your wings. If you confirm that you are ready, you take a additional flap to get this level of preparation. When you are ready then you open your wings and fly. Get up and be calm. awake as an aspiring daydreamer.

Chapter 3: Leaps Of Failures To Climb

"There is only one thing that makes a dream impossible to achieve: the fear of failure." Paulo Coelho. Paulo Coelho

Are you afraid to fail? As you are, the majority individuals are. It's normal to be nervous at the point where you're forming your vision creating it, defining it, and then claiming the dream. It's perfectly normal to be scared.

Perhaps you'd like to revisit the fundamental question: what is it that makes us so scared of failing? Hypnotherapist certified Tellman Knudson explains,

"In my time in the field of hypnotherapy, something has been made obvious: ask a typical person what they're doing wrong to not achieve their objectives yet. The the fear of failing will come up as the top barrier to achieving success for the majority people most times.

Why is this? There are many motives. It is interesting to note that they do not have anything to do with having a parent lacking self-confidence. It is all to do with the fear of being rejected as a socially accepted behavior."

Whatever you're, an adult who is fearful of taking bolder decisions because it could impact the whole family, an aspiring young person or woman looking to find where you fit in the world. We all experience that tension every time we consider our hopes in public and are looking forward to doing something to reach our goals.

Here's a powerful story that was shared by a life coach Yvette Bowlin

"I myself push through my periods of feeling defeated. For instance, I was a treasurer of the student body in seventh grade but lost to my adversaries. Also, when I was dismissed from my first job following graduation from college. In particular, when I had to dissolve my two-year-old company that was bankrupt at the beginning of 2008's recession.

There's nothing to do.

Then, at the time of finishing senior high school, I became with the title of valedictorian. A few weeks after losing my job, I was able to employment with a business that seemed to be a more suitable one for my talents and temperament. After putting my company after which I returned to college, obtaining my Masters at Business Administration, and graduated with a distinction.

In my inability to realize how failing could really benefit me, I believed I'd lost my way in those traumatic moments. Each event felt tragic. Yet, I was able to realize the other things to enjoy after the first doors had closed.

In retrospect, I can see everything was fine. every thing that took place.

Would we have this retrospective view, even in the midst of difficult circumstances? Shouldn't it make our lives less painful (if it wasn't enjoyable)?

Opportunities that came up from the lack of success resulted in what I had hoped for prior to it pale in comparison with what I ultimately received. It was just a matter of being determined to watch it happen."

Yvette is one among many on the market who share stories of challenges as ladders. We live in a culture that emphasizes success, don't be distracted by the beauty of failures. It is possible to find the stories of these kinds and be so enthralled. The biggest stars you admire be able to tell this story. to share.

As you progress, you'll discover those gems that are hidden within mistakes. This might not be the easiest thing to master but let move and you can lead you to success. Consider failure as stepping up the steps. Relax in the fact that you're not failing simply because you're not willing to give up so easily. Your vulnerability is human, and will not be judged on your flawlessness. Each failure is a ladder to climb - one that makes you rise higher, expand your reach. Each failure can be a cleanse. The way to look at failures is in this manner:

A) They help you become stronger. Many authors have written on how the scars or the splinters we experience due to failures may give way into light, to understanding. Consider every loss as learning experience. The experience of failure can create a mark on your psyche, however it'll be seen as a sign of faith and determination. They are similar to maps which will only take us to more desirable locations.

(b) These can take you on the right path. It's possible to look at it as follows: if you fail at anything, no matter what you do it, it might be an opportunity to think about it again and consider another route towards the goal you've always wanted to achieve. Take a closer look at your voice to discover its true sound. In the event that we do not succeed to speak, it's as if the wind vane was pointed towards an opposite direction.

If you are feeling anxious, you, take a moment to settle to yourself by reminding yourself this feelings of fear are temporary. Don't let your mistakes define yourself. Be aware that failure is commonplace and, generally individuals can connect to it in the core of their own souls.

If you are scared of your goals, it can will only indicate how much would like to pursue them to see them come true.

Chapter 4: Motivation To Inspire You

"Failure is an integral part of the path to success. Anyone who is averse to failure will do not have success." Robert T. Kiyosaki

Do you recall the times when you read about an individual's story of success and having the ability to realize their goals? Did you recall how your heart gave into and you were so in awe? The best way to motivate yourself to take steps is to keep yourself motivated. Through this section of the book allow yourself to be enthralled by the inspiring words of those who took action and fulfilled their goals.

The stories of people who followed the call of their souls guide you on your own path.

* Mahatma Gandhi

This is probably the most inspiring story. Barrister by birth in India as a trade, he did not appear to be a great lawyer because it was difficult for him to cross-check witnesses. After some time spent writing lawsuit letters, he moved on a trip to South Africa where he developed his skills as a politician. This was no cakewalk for him, and his Satyagraha protests were awash by difficulties, even within India. The most notable failure ever was the division of India as well as Pakistan.

In the present, he's among the most sought-after and powerful leaders in the history of humanity. The youngest of us know what he's like.

* J.K. Rowling

J.K. Rowling, the writer of the Harry Potter novels was waitressing and receiving public assistance while she began writing the initial book in what would later turn out to be the best-selling books in the history of literature. The novel was rejected by more than a dozen publishers. The reason why it was released was that the CEO's 8 year girl daughter asked for him to publish the book.

J.K. is just one of many single mothers struggling in order to meet their financial needs and pursue their own desires while pursuing their children's goals. If she gave up, we might not have been able to enjoy this science fiction entertainment.

* Henry Ford

The first two Ford automobile firms were unsuccessful. This didn't prevent him from creating the Ford Motor Company and being the first person to introduce manufacturing on assembly lines to manufacturing affordable cars across the globe. He did not just revolutionize the manufacturing process of Europe and the United States and Europe, however, he also had a significant impact in the development of 20th century economics and the society.

He is now one of the most well-known people not only within the automotive industry but in across the whole archive of worldwide-recognized achievements.

* Michael Jordan

"I am averaging more than 9000 shots during my professional time. I've lost nearly 300 games. In 26 instances, I've been assigned to shoot the shot that would win the game, but I failed. My failures have been repeated repeatedly in my career. This is the reason I am successful."

Who isn't familiar with who is this NBA player? Everyone who hasn't seen his game on television knows who he really is. He is admired by many not only for his skills in sports, but also for his story of life as well as his "never say die" spirit.

* Vincent van Gogh

The man was manic depression. He was unable to function for in half of the time. There was no success for him in his time, however his work has been regarded as the best painting painted by anyone in the world. In consequence his name has become an appeal to artists from all over the world that have repeatedly been rejected and overlooked.

He has touched the lives of so many and has paved the way for acceptance and appreciation of the his uniqueness.

* Walt Disney

Disney established his own company in his garage at home, and his first animated production was a failure. At his press meeting, a journalist mocked Walt Disney because he had no ideas on how to go about film production.

Disney is an American film director, producer as well as screenwriter, voice actor and animator. One of the most famous motion picture producers around the entire world. Disney created a film production firm. The company, which is now referred to as the 'The Walt Disney Company' generates an annual revenues of US 30 billion annually.

* Steve Jobs

He was 30 years old and in a state of depression and despair when he was abruptly removed from the firm he created, Apple, after a battle against the directors back in 1985. Then, he bought the company's computer graphics division from Lucasfilm and was able to get the cash required to take back control of Apple.

His story and words has inspired many both old and young.

* Marilyn Monroe

In 1947, just one year into her contract Marilyn Monroe was dropped by 20th Century-Fox because her producer considered her unattractive and could not be seen as attractive enough. That didn't deter her at all! The actress kept going until eventually, she was recognized by the general public as being the most famous 20th century film star, sex icon and pop star.

* Albert Einstein

In his early years, Albert Einstein had some difficulties communicating and learning according to the traditional way. However, Einstein's communication and behavioral issues weren't necessarily indicative of low intellect. Einstein won the Nobel Prize in physics for his discovery of the photoelectric effect. his unique theory of relativity theory redressed the shortcomings of Newtonian Physics.

These are the greatest crowdfunding success tales that will give you the impression that you're a normal individual, you are still able to achieve the top when you are convinced of your vision and then do something about it:

* How a small group of students led to transformation in the biggest city in Ghana

In the year that David Boyd travelled to Ghana as a judicial human rights assignment, he witnessed firsthand the issues faced by thousands of people who live in the slums Old Fadama. Particularly, he observed that the inaccessibility of electric power was creating havoc for people living in the area, as dangerous electrical fires regularly ruining homes of thousands. After returning to home, Boyd set out to develop an answer. Boyd began to form a group made up of his fellow students, and Energy for Old Fadama was created.

Two years later, having the PS17,000 they raised from a crowdfunding campaign, as well as the additional funds raised from investors, the team of students of Energy for Old Fadama are getting close towards achieving their goal of transforming Ghana's biggest urban slum.

This is an excellent instance of collective success. When you declare your goal and set out to achieve it, chances for the success you desire open up. The project might start with one individual, however his belief in his own goals has touched a lot of lives to this day.

* How the band raised money to finance an album that could transform the lives of people

Melodime started a campaign on an online crowdfunding platform to help fund their forthcoming album. The proceeds of the album will be donated to a charity that provides the instruments for free and also music education for children with the same love to music as their great-grandfather had - kids who may not be capable of affording the purchase of an instrument.

The power of kindness can help dreamers to go further. They make a significant difference to the lives of people who are unable to afford their musical dreams. When we express our ideas across the globe and create an impact. This is an example you can take with you and pull the best ideas from.

* What happened when Mikey Leung sought help to present Bangladesh in a new light

Mikey is a Sydney-based graphic designer videographer and storyteller from Sydney who is passionate for the country and people of Bangladesh. He was exhausted by the fact with the fact that what you read about Bangladesh is negativity including flooding and poverty. He was determined to tell the story of Bangladesh which he is familiar with as a place that is full of colors and artwork beautiful natural beauty, and very accommodating people. He's driven to tell this positive tale in order to inspire others to go to Bangladesh which will create jobs and openings.

"We discovered the real chance for travel in this country to serve as a means to generate an economic opportunity for those who need it as well as to bring about transformation in Bangladesh. There wasn't a specific title for it initially and then it changed to Crowdsourced Travel after we realized that we had to open it up as an initiative, an opportunity for individuals to gather to solve this problem using whatever ideas or resources they had to share at each other."

This tale simply illustrates the way we can imagine both for ourselves and others. Do you have this same dream? There are more people who dream of becoming a dreamer that you could imagine.

Here are a handful of the numerous inspirational stories that are ready to motivate you. Also, you can visit the following websites to encourage you, and to remind you that you're nearing the point of achieving the goals you have set for yourself:

* TED Talks

* Tiny Buddha

* Zen Habits

It's all about inspiration. It doesn't matter if it's a renowned successful story or something else any thing you are able to take into consideration that could set your to ablaze is genuinely beneficial. If you've got an open mind and heart, you will come across the most inspirational and inspirational stories.

Harvard Business Review wrote this incredible article on the power of inspiration.

In a world focused on measuring the quality of talent and capability and assessing talent, we tend to overlook the importance of inspiracion. Inspiring us with the possibilities of the future by permitting us to go beyond our normal situations and limits. Inspiring people to move from being apathetic to awe and alters how we see our potential. It is sometimes neglected due to its inaccessible nature. The way it's been treated as divine or supernatural can be a hindrance. As recent studies have shown the power of inspiration is stimulated, gathered, and controlled, which can have a significant impact on crucial life events.

If you are offline you are, there are a million reasons to be invigorated by. Keep in mind that this is a amazing flow of life.

Here are some easy ways to be inspired by your surroundings:

1.) Take a stroll. Walking in the woods clears your mind and keep you focused on those things that matter most to you in life.

2) Watch children play. Children are among the most attentive of all. They are present and are not afraid. Let their energy flow through them.

3.) Be attentive to your pet when you go for a stroll. As with children, pet's minds are alert. They are free to roam around.

4.) Take a deep breath and listening to the natural sound surrounding you.

Imagine the beautiful oceans and bodies of water that link two continents in one place to another. Imagine the multitude of people like you who are also struggling to fulfill their goals outside, only to find out that the dream is actually inside them.

You know what you're seeking is within your. So, feel it. Take a bath and then get involved.

Chapter 5: Your Flame

The book for children is easy to read and yet it is a feast for the mind and heart. The story is about one boy named Ax who wishes to blow flames (like dragons) in order to unleash his power. In his mind Ax met a dragon friend, who took him to the land of Dragons. A few days ago, he asked his friend to not fight against other tiny dragons since they could actually be best close even though they are differently. He awoke in the arms of his Mother and she says to himthat "your inner fire is your big open heart and it makes me proud!"

There is an inner fire that is unique to you.

Your inner fire will always inspire you to take action in achieving your goals.

We all have times when we get so shaky and depressed. We all need confirmation. How can you handle this? Do you have to fight it against it, or simply try focus your attention on something positive and fun?

These are a few ways will help you stay connected to your passion:

Reminisce about the ways you've fought for your goals through the years.

As a young person there were also obstacles while trying to achieve the goals you've set. Think back to those experiences and the way you managed to accomplish every item on your list of buckets. Reminding yourself constantly of the power you have to endure and accomplish something can be an effective fuel. Even though you were older, you were aware of how much frustration and hurt could feel to be. However, you resolutely got up and carried on. Do you have that picture in your mind of the day that you prevailed over the fall. That will help you imagine and dream again.

- Examine your core at the time you're in need of it most

At your lowest the moment, you must shut out all other noise as well as you, and place your focus in your center. The truth is that you are a person by God with a special brightness and light. Be aware of that and feel the peace you seek in your own radiant light. The dreams you have are within you and nobody else will erase that. That's what you should be looking for when you are feeling down or away from your dream.

* Look through you feel the pain and the suffering of waiting

Make it a habit to imagine you rising above suffering, pain, and even failure. It will help you stay safe and help you believe when you are facing the toughest of situations. The truth is that you are capable of doing far more than you thought of. Keep in mind that the word "problem" does not have to mean the rest of your existence. There are memories you have accumulated that look beautiful, and you've fulfilled your aspirations before (that have been long dreams). This is the reason you're in a position to overcome and triumph against pain.

Do not be afraid to count on your nearest circle

We all become vulnerable at moments. In these instances don't be scared to admit your vulnerability whenever you require help. It's perfectly acceptable to reach out to your circle of support including family, friends as well as counsellors, to offer your more time, patience and support in times when you require it most. Did you call a loved one at those most difficult hours, only to cry over the line that came up? Go do it. You'll be perfect. It happens. There are times when you have to make calls. At times, you answer the phone. It's wonderful to hear. There are many giving people. You can be a receiver and come fully circle.

* Fuel your fire in the outside and also

Are you aware that if you feel insecure inner side, you can also find yourself feeling weak and tired on the outside? If, for instance, you're experiencing a difficult time of sadness, it is also apparent that you are losing the appetite and vitality. Don't get carried away. You must feed your inner fire, too. Take a healthy diet, take some rest, meditate and exercise. It's important to remain fit and healthy to avoid make you feel unbalanced. In scientific terms, you're not superhuman and may become weak and ill. Be sure to take care of yourself even on the toughest times.

* Seek out positive influences and be absorbed by it

The great thing about being who you are now is that you hold the ability to decide the people around you. As you work towards your goals, ensure that you surround yourself with positive people and positivity. Avoid spending time with people that are negative and can make you feel tired and demotivated.

If you are feeling that you don't have enough positive influence around you take a trip to the library and other sources like movies and music. Follow the example of the role models they have, they could help you out when you require the most.

• Keep a file of happy reminders you will be able to use

This file will be your go-to spot whenever you are feeling like your goals aren't as big. These include messages that express appreciation and beautiful phrases that inspire your spirit and help you remember how you can achieve your goals. If you feel energized, it is also possible to be able to feel the light coming from your insides. You can feel potential.

* Allow the endorphins to assist you in making decisions

What made you feel so satisfied at times in the past (and it never stopped making you feel more energized)? Think of the moments you felt so delighted and engage in these things over and over. Happy hormones and endorphins can increase our mood, and allow us appreciate the good aspects of the world. If you can remember having a great time playing guitar, walking along with your pal or making breakfast, make it happen. The good and the hay makes people want to fantasize about!

• Get involved with something important

Certain people are able to see the value doing volunteer work or participate in a volunteer effort in the community. It is because these experiences and connections give the feeling of satisfaction and feeling of connection. In these experiences where we can begin to think about our dreams, not only to ourselves, but for other people too.

You can strengthen your spiritual connection

It is a fact that you are a dreamer as you embody this amazing universe. Build and maintain your connection to the divine as this is a important way to gain an idea of what direction you're headed in the pursuit of your dreams. Meditate. Keep your attention.

This is a routine that you could also do to help remind you of the fire within you:

- Find a place that is ideal to spend time with your loved ones. You can find peace and focus on breathing.

Recall and reflect on your favorite traits in you.

"One at a time, take them in your mind. Each one at a time. Breathe slowly, deep.

You can breathe slowly, and visualize it as an affirmation to show you're solid.

Repeat the process until you are at ease and happy.

Beginning this exercise early in the morning, or at anytime you've got some extra time to yourself can greatly assist to keep you on track in your goals.

Sometimes, you may be distracted. Sometimes, you may feel exhausted or unable on certain moments. However, as long as you direct your focus and energy into the goals you'd like to reach and do what you can to achieve it the things you want to achieve, your heart shines in unending light.

Chapter 6: Your Circle Of Support

Prior to this, you've been advised to depend on your close friends for help. In this chapter, we'll explore the significance of your circle of support. Then, we'll go further to appreciate the importance of family members, friends as well as other significant people around the world today.

The entire family

While the times have changed but it isn't a secret that having the love and support from our loved ones is unparalleled. It is possible to have unique situations or scenarios that don't permit us to get assistance from their support. But If you do have them in your life right now don't hesitate to depend on your family members. Family members are among your closest circle of friends that you can depend on.

When you're trying to implement your goals, they're here to remind you that it is possible to achieve them. A family dinner could be the perfect opportunity for discussing your dreams. You can talk with them and become more open and may even talk about your enthusiasm and anxieties. Your family members know you've grown and are able to give good suggestions on the most important aspects you need to think about.

In case you're living close to a farm or family, why not spend longer with your family?

Dear Friends

Everyone knows that items we don't want to reveal to our families, we are able to divulge it to our close friends. Friendship can be a great source of inspiration for us in different ways. Because the majority of our friends are similar age, it's much easier to talk about our most intimate anxieties and secret. When you're on the path to actions to realize your dream It is always a good idea having a support system of people who encourage you when you're feeling low, and will be able to give you honest advice on how to proceed.

Being able to have friends connect with your dream makes the process enjoyable and fun. If you're just declaring the goals you have set or making them a reality and have friends to help you make it easier. They're our cheerleaders and constructive criticism. We learn from them, and want to share our achievements with them too.

Other significant

The person you share the journey with is a key player during this adventure. The same dream you have is theirs. Being able to count on a friend to support you can mean much. There is someone who can comfort yourself when you are low; and there is someone you can be with during times when you feel like the dream is so close. If you're stressed you can count on someone to support your soul. If you can share the highs and lows of your journey it is more energizing to enjoy every step of the process - regardless of no matter how great, or the contrary. What's more gorgeous than to have someone stand to you, no matter how difficult?

Be aware that you need to be honest as you are able to be with your spouse. By remaining open and honest you will have more space to communicate, and a greater relationship and understanding between you, as well as how you can best work together in order to realize your goals.

The writer Amanda Chatel shares, "a recent study from Washington University in St. Louis discovered that the persona of one spouse can significantly impact the performance of the partner. For a time period of five years five thousand married couples with ages ranging from 19 to 89, had their career paths studied. Researchers weighed the effects of their salary, the satisfaction they had with the job and how often they got elevated, and discovered that couples with supportive spouses had a higher chance of success in their work and more determined. People in relationships with problems and who were at risk of poor work performance."

To ensure that you get the most out of your group support make note of these important reminders

Open your mind and heart.

"Make your ego porous. Will has no value complaining about nothing. popularity isn't anything. Flexibility, patience, and openness and solitude are the most important things."

-- Rainer Maria Rilke

When you travel towards your goal, you'll encounter challenges and pitfalls. Don't take anything as a cause for bitterness. Let your thoughts be known with anyone who make up your support group. It's impossible to predict who could help you clarify your thoughts and bring back that sense of wanting to strive the goals you have set for yourself.

As an example, perhaps you have a dream of being a teacher. At some moment, you realize like you've found a distinct passion. At some point in your path, you decide to decide to quit and go off the beaten path. Speak it to a person in your circle of friends. Inform them of your situation and maybe they could offer you tips.

Be attentive to their needs regardless of how determined to achieve your goals

If you are ablaze, it is possible that you will forget about someone else's emotions. The people you love, your family members, and your significant other also have ambitions of their own. There are times when your priorities might be at odds or they may not show the same level of attention to you. Be more open-minded and perseverant. When you are taking the steps towards your goals make sure you are there for other people also. What is more rewarding than helping one another achieve success? The saying goes, "Happiness is the most genuine when it's shared.

• Express your gratitude throughout the day.

Don't forget to thank you to the people who support you. Whatever you are able to tell how much or little they have done to you, show them your appreciation. Remember that the path towards your goals will not be easier without them to help you. Even in the most difficult situations try to cultivate gratitude within your soul. An open heart that allows for gratitude will never go out of its path. This is an excellent quote of Umass Education about gratitude:

The study of happiness and the state of mind that it brings, is gaining popularity within psychological as well as scientific research (it is long been a popular topic in the areas of philosophy and religion) There is a growing amount of study of the nature and characteristics of gratefulness, the causes and the potential implications in terms of health and well-being mental/emotional. In this piece, I'll examine some of the latest discoveries about the link with gratitude, health and well-being as well as outline methods to improve the sense and express gratitude throughout your daily life.

When you are guided to gratitude by the spirit of God, your heart opens and is open to many kinds of good fortune. A heart that is grateful opens to the possibility of dreams. The pursuit of dreams can lead to happiness and the love of your life.

* Be inspired and invigorate yourself

You have the potential to inspire other people as well as you could motivate you. This reservoir of inspiration should guide you to the direction of your dreams. Family, friends as well as your partner can provide you with inspiration in many different ways. They can teach you determination from them all as they also live their lives every day, and pursuing their own ambitions and dreams. Also, you can gain courage from them because when they go about their daily lives They put aside fear to make sure that all things as well as everyone else around them is aligned with their personal goals.

Here's a daily routine you can follow so that you're always improving your connections to your group of support:

* Locate a calm place where you will be able to experience tranquility

* Close your eyes, and focus upon your breath.

Consider the amazing relationships and people within your current life.

* While you are thinking of the different ones, breathe into your lungs and exhale at a steady pace.

* Make sure you have a clear picture of your community support group, and begin to thank you when you breathe out.

The simple exercise of meditation will help you reconnect with the amazing nature of support as well as being taken care of and having people around to cheer you on to your accomplishments.

Chapter 7: Believing In Yourself

"Faith is taking the first step even when you don't see the whole staircase." Martin Luther King Jr.

It's been a wonderful trip for you. Each time you take a page from the book, you become more likely to take actions; reaching to grab the dream by the palms of your fingers. Imagine the day that an idea erupted in your head. You were so excited and delighted, didn't you? The dream grew until it got bigger, and you started to experience a feeling of anxiety.

However you continued to dream. You began to imagine what it appears, what it felt. And then, you reached the feeling of acknowledging it as your own, and taking the whole thing into. While you feel ownership of it as a feeling, you think about the numerous inspirations that will help you in achieving the goal. Each step you take in your journey and every contribution which can help make it happen.

Failures were seen with a new perspective - they became something that makes your character stronger and more wise. Your attitude towards life is also changing as you have become more open. Every moment there's a small miraculous event, your heart gets warmer and you are unable to feel thankful. That's how a happy mind performs well - it lives through faith, potential and gratitude.

Now is the time to act. The day is now when your goals will free you and allow you to fly. To do that it is essential to possess sufficient confidence. You are today more of the person you really are. There is no one who can stop your progress because you've been able to love yourself and you're enjoying the sweet benefits of this affection.

What's the importance of the faith we have in our lives? What is the importance of faith when it comes to taking actions?

It's faith that makes you go. Faith helps you be able to see light in the darkness. It's faith that helps calm your mind when you're stressed and unwilling to trust. The greater force of goodwill is waiting for you in times of stress. It's that sweet light of hope that gets you up every early morning, slowly but gently. While others may quit on your potential, faith is your voice to let you know that you are able to keep going. The same excitement that keeps you going when you take a one step towards your most important ambition. If no one will be watching, it's the faith of yours that carries the same passion as you do, it is convinced of the possibility of a brighter tomorrow. This is the kind of thing you can find in the tales of struggles and joy from other people including your family members, friends and your loved ones. This is the message that knocks at your doorstep when you are dreading dawns and the beginning of a new day. It's what causes you to weep in genuine joy when you hear someone say, "I am with you all the way!"

It is not a shape. It isn't even a thing. colours. You'll find it even in the most unimaginable locations. If you're in the area, will be. This is the factor that connects people regardless of the odds. It is for a boy who was young, it's gravity which makes him go ahead, and for those who have lost their lives, the renewal of their lives. It's the key ingredient which helps people who are old to discover meaning in even small items.

If you're in the midst of a downturn and despair, it's the thought to get back up and take on the challenge or embarrassment. When you are in a state of vulnerability the reminder lets you enjoy the fragility and allows you to move toward claiming success, improvement, and success.

If you are asked "why don't you quit?" Faith can make you laugh in awe and then answer "just because."

Think about this:

When you trust in yourself, you have a dream to share with the incredible women and men who came through your path: Einstein, Jordan, Jobs and many other unknown heroes that have created revolution, breakthrough as well as love and transformation into our lives right now. Are you able to believe the magnitude of this is? Faith has always been everywhere throughout your life. Right before your birth. This is how amazing it can be. It's an incredible power...inexorable.

Every day, make the effort to take steps towards your goals. Allow the rhythm of your life to lead you. Everything is going so effortlessly even though it's chaotic.

How do you go about taking the necessary steps and achieve your goals?

• Follow your instincts

"Our body has five senses: touch taste, smell as well as hearing, sight and smell. However, not to be ignored are the senses that make up our souls, such as perception, peace and foresight. They also have trust as well as compassion. What makes them different is their capacity to use these senses the majority of people do not have any knowledge of the inner senses, while some depend upon them in the same manner as much as they depend on the physical sense or perhaps greater." C. Joybell C. Joybell C.

Have ever heard that tiny voice that says which direction to take every time? It's that tiny energy which whispers your initial decisions and your reactions. In some cases, and even most times the person who is following the advice due to anxiety. Now more than ever, you need to listen to it and pay attention. Faithful people know what their desires are. Realizing your goals is just near the edge of your intuition. Like you've had the experience of You'll be afraid, make a decision because of your fear, only to afterwards, you'll regret the decision.

Don't be afraid to change your mind.

"Life is a full circle, widening until it joins the circle motion of the infinite."

The dreams will never be only dreams if you're not acting on them gradually, one at a time. Dreams are lovely and can be made your dreams come true. What are you wasting time to do? This is the perfect opportunity to get moving; to realize one goal at a time, and then be able to share it with your family, friends and to the people around the world. Thoughts without action will disappear with the passing of the years. Since the world changes quicker than it ever has the past, don't be surprised if your never-fulfilled wish will be realized someday - only that from someone else. Move. Make a move in good faith. You can do it.

One action can lead to a different one. Start with optimism and do to avoid getting back to square one.

Be humble

"A great man is always willing to be little."
-- Ralph Waldo Emerson

If you are at the point when you're taking action in pursuit of your dream keep in mind to remain humble. There is a tendency to be overwhelmed by the exhilaration and excitement of seeing the unfolding of your goals before your eyes. Allow humility to live within your heart and mind and you will stay in a steady place. This is the kind of humility that keeps you feel connected to your community. When you lower your self-esteem to see things clearly You can sense people more clearly and live your life in the joy and gratitude.

Are you aware that those who are most successful tend to be less modest? This is due to the fact that they've had to go through so much in their lives, and their knowledge has enlightened their lives. Whatever challenge you face, remember that you're not big... nevertheless, you are important.

Please share your experience with friends and family.

"Vulnerability is the source of connection, and it is also the way to a feeling of satisfaction. If the sharing doesn't make you feel vulnerable it's likely to be beneficial."

When you walk and run do you not have the time to be open to sharing your sorrows and joys with other people? The vulnerability you share will not just enable you, but also others; it can also heal. Sharing is what makes the world go around. When you set your sights on your goals, you're encouraging others to pursue their own. If you are able to share the wisdom and the beauty of failing as well as shedding your light on to the community as well as the entire world. Nobody is an isle. There's nothing more satisfying than sharing the breadth of humankind with others. the joy, the sorrow the glory.

When you make a decision take action, remember that the entire world is cheering with you.

And, when you have all these tools and words that help you to discover your personal goals and pursue these, how do you resist? Consider this opportunity. Consider it as if it could disappear at any time. When it comes to dancing, do it as if no one is listening.

Let me give you a few suggestions to help you sleep:

The impossible dream to fantasy

For the fight against an unbeatable opponent

The pain of unimaginable grief

to run in places where brave would rather not

In order to correct the inexplicably wrong

To be a lover of pure and clean from far

You can try it when your arms have become tired

In order to reach the star that is not accessible

It is the reason I am here.

In order to follow the star

Whatever the outcome

However you travel

In order to fight for what is right

In the absence of pause or question

Be willing to walk towards Hell

To support a noble reason

If I'm honest, I'm honest, it will be

This is a glorious journey

In my heart, I will be in peace and tranquil

As I lay to my relaxation

and the world will be a better place for it.

One man was who was scorned, covered with scars and tattered.

But he fought to the end with just one inch of strength

To get to the inaccessible star

Chapter 8: Setting And Achieving Goals

We will focus on the necessity of establishing clearly defined goals and the part that actions play in the pursuit of these objectives. There are a variety of strategies and methods you could employ to achieve your goals. This includes developing goals that are SMART by breaking bigger objectives into more manageable, smaller activities, and creating an action plan.

A key element in the process of the definition and achievement of objectives is setting SMART objectives. The SMART goals are specific Goals that are Measurable and Achievable that are relevant and time-bound. When you set goals that are in line with these traits, you will ensure that your objectives are precise, achievable and achievable.

As well as defining SMART targets, it's essential to separate larger objectives into smaller, more achievable goals. This will allow you to focus on achieving your goals by taking small steps at a time instead of feeling overwhelmed by your larger goals. When you tackle small tasks to build momentum, you will be able to move forward and progress toward the ultimate goal.

A crucial aspect of achieving your goals is to have an action plan. It involves determining the specific tasks you must complete to reach the goals you have set, and establishing the timeframe for accomplishing the assignments. If you have a strategy established, you will be able to stay focused and motivated as you strive to achieve your goals.

The process of setting and achieving goals is an effective method of focusing your efforts and energy to what's most important to us and help us bring our dreams and hopes to completion. There are several essential elements of setting and achieving targets:

1.Clearly identify your goals The most important thing is to spend the time to write down your goal, as well as what you're hoping to achieve as well as what is most essential for you. This can help make sure that your goals align to your ideals and values.

2.Make your goals clear and quantifiable. Goals that are specific and quantifiable are easier to achieve and to track progress towards. As an example you could instead state the goal of "exercise more," you could set yourself a target to "exercise for 30 minutes, three times each week."

3.Create real-world goals that are achievable and attainable 3. Create realistic and achievable goals: It's important to establish goals that are not only not easy, but are also achievable and achievable. It will ensure you're able to achieve your goals and feel an overall feeling of accomplishment while working towards the goals you have set.

4.Construct strategies and start taking action. Once you've established your goals and goals, you must make a plan to achieve the goals. This could involve breaking down the goals into manageable, smaller assignments and setting deadlines to meet your goals. Also, it is essential to work towards your goals on a regular basis. This is the only way to help in achieving your goals and achieve your goals.

5.Evaluate the progress you have made and adjust your plan if needed When you are working towards your goals, it's important to monitor your progress, and then evaluate whether you're in the right direction to achieve the goals. If you're not seeing the progress you would like It is important to adjust your plan and adjust it to help keep you on the right course.

In order to achieve your goals, you must having clear objectives by making them specific and measurable, establishing attainable and achievable targets, creating strategies and then taking actions while reviewing the performance and revising the plan according to the needs. Following these steps to create goals and achieve them, as well as bring your dreams and dreams to reality.

The overall goal of this chapter is to give you the tools and techniques you'll need to establish and achieve your goals, as well as be successful in your pursuit.

Chapter 9: Overcoming Procrastination And Self-Doubt

The most common challenges associated with procrastination and self-doubt. How doing something about it can assist you in overcoming these challenges. This article will examine the fundamental motivations behind procrastination as well as self-doubt while discussing methods and strategies are available to help overcame these issues and move forward towards your objectives.

Procrastination is a problem which many of us face which can pose an obstacle in achieving your objectives. Procrastination is caused by many factors such as inability to motivate yourself, fear of failing, or inability to focus or maintain discipline. To combat procrastination, it's important to determine the root cause behind the procrastination you are experiencing and then take steps to tackle the issue. This could mean setting clearly defined objectives, breaking more complex tasks into smaller and simpler steps, or requesting help and accountable.

The fear of self-doubt is a common obstacle which can prevent you from making a move and reaching the goals you set. It can result from an insecurity or fear of failing, or even a negative attitude. In order to overcome self-doubt it is crucial to work on building confidence, changing negative beliefs as well as seeking out support and encouragement from other people.

Self-doubt and procrastination can become significant obstacles in achieving our objectives and leading an enjoyable life. Procrastination involves put off or postponing work or obligations, usually because of feelings of overwhelming and lack of motivation or fear of failing. Self-doubt can be defined as a lack of confidence in one's skills or worthiness, which may cause feeling of uncertainty and fear. Here are some suggestions for dealing with self-doubt, procrastination, and putting:

1.Set specific goals and prioritizes Setting specific goals and objectives can assist in focusing your attention and effort, making it simpler to act. It also helps alleviate feelings of overwhelming and uncertainty because you understand what you're striving for and why it is crucial to you.

2.Break jobs into manageable, smaller steps: Big, overwhelming projects can seem stressful and cause delay. If you break down tasks into smaller, manageable steps, you will be able to make improvements more quickly and avoid anxiety.

3.Identify and confront negative thinking patterns: Self-doubt can stem in negative thoughts, like "I can't do this" or "I'm not good enough." If you can identify and challenge those thoughts, you will be able to change your perspective and gain confidence in your capabilities.

4.Seek help and encouragers A good idea is to get support and motivation from family members, friends, or even a coach when you are struggling with doubts about yourself. Being surrounded by a network of support can increase your self-confidence and boost determination, as well as provide the motivation you need in times of need.

5.Take small steps, and then celebrate your accomplishments: It's essential to acknowledge your accomplishments regardless of how little because it will help to boost confidence and increase determination. Through small, incremental steps and recognizing your accomplishments throughout the process to build up momentum and conquer procrastination and doubt about yourself.

Overcoming self-doubt and procrastination requires making clear your goals as well as priorities. It also involves breaking projects into manageable steps, challenging the negative thoughts patterns getting support and motivation by taking tiny steps while celebrating your accomplishments. With these tips and techniques, you will be able to conquer the obstacles that stand in your way and reach your objectives with confidence and conviction

Chapter 10: The Importance Of Planning And Prioritizing

It is crucial to plan and prioritizing are essential components to success in achieving your goals. This article explores various tactics and methods you can employ to organize and prioritize your work and obligations, and maximize your time and funds.

Planning and prioritizing effectively requires prioritizing your objectives and the activities and tasks needed to accomplish the targets. This also requires creating an agenda or schedule that assists you in allocating your resources and time to allow you to be focused on your primary assignments and obligations. Through planning and prioritizing the tasks and duties you have to perform will ensure you're making progress toward the goals you have set and maximize the efficiency of your work.

There are a variety of methods and strategies can be used to organize and prioritize your work and duties. They include making a to-do schedule, establishing priority as well as time blockers. The to-do list will help you organize and identify the things you'll need to finish, and making priorities helps you be focused on the most important projects prior to anything else. Time blocking involves breaking the day up into segments of time, and assigning specific assignments or activities for each block. This will help you focus and keep your attention on the task at hand.

Prioritizing and planning are crucial techniques for succeeding and living a fulfilled life. They assist us in focusing the focus of our efforts and energy to what matters most for us and to assure us that we're getting closer to our goals. Below are some methods of prioritizing and planning is beneficial.

1. Increases productivity and efficiency Through creating a strategy and prioritizing our work and obligations, we will become more efficient and productive both in our professional and life in general. It can allow us to maximize the time we have and our resources and accomplish the goals we set more efficiently and efficiently.

2. Helps to decrease anxiety and stress: Prioritizing and planning can assist in reducing feelings of anxiety and stress by offering the structure and clarity. When we know what must be accomplished and at what time it is possible to be more in control of our lives, as well as better equipped to manage the pressures and difficulties that may come to us.

3.Improves the process of making decisions: Planning and prioritizing are also a way in improving decision-making because it allows us to think about the long-term implications of our choices and to make decisions that align with our values and goals.

Prioritizing and planning are essential abilities that increase efficiency as well as lessen anxiety and stress, improve the motivation and focus, and enhance the quality of decisions. If we take the time to organize and prioritize the tasks and obligations we have it is possible to meet the goals we set and lead an enjoyable and fulfilling life.

In the end, this chapter will give you the tools and techniques you require to prioritize and plan your responsibilities and tasks as well as to move toward your objectives effectively and efficiently. method.

Chapter 11: Building Habits And Consistency

The significance of habits and consistency when it comes to taking actions and reaching your objectives. This session will look at the psychology of habits and the ways they influence your behaviour and choices, as well as we discuss methods and strategies which you can employ to develop solid habits and create the habit of consistency throughout your everyday life.

Habits are automatic behavior patterns that trigger by events or cues. They play a major role that affects our lives because they affect our behavior and behaviours in a predictable and predictable manner. When you establish positive habits you will be able to build a solid foundation to take action and make improvements towards achieving your goals.

In order to build positive habits, it's important to determine your specific actions that will be transformed into routines and then make a plan to incorporate the actions you want to incorporate into your daily routine. This could include setting certain time frames or triggers to accomplish the desired tasks in addition to seeking help and accountability from your friends.

Consistency is an additional aspect in developing good habits and reaching the goals you set. If you are consistent in pursuing your objectives, you will achieve momentum and growth, and remain focused and motivated in your pursuit of success.

Establishing habits and being consistent is essential to being successful and leading an enjoyable life. Habits are the actions occur regularly and are automatic that can result in significant influence on our lives as well as overall health. Consistency refers to maintaining consistency in the way we conduct ourselves and our behaviors which is an essential element in the development and maintenance of the habits we have developed.

Enhances productivity and efficiency Habits enable us to complete actions and tasks without needing to think about them constantly and can boost the efficiency and productivity of our lives. When we develop habits that are in line with our ideals and beliefs and values, we will be able to improvements more efficiently and quickly.

Increases self-control and discipline Making habits takes self-control and discipline. This is because we have to be committed to executing the desired behaviour regularly over the course of the course of. When we develop these habits that we develop, we will increase our self-control and improve our discipline, as well as be more able to reach our goals and reach the potential we have.

Improves self-confidence and confidence Congruity in our behavior and actions increases our confidence as well as self-esteem by proving our self and other individuals that we're competent and trustworthy.

Improves happiness and well-being: Making habits to support our wellbeing, like engaging in regular physical activity or practicing gratitude, will improve the overall happiness and well-being of our lives.

creating habits and a consistent approach are essential to being successful and leading an enjoyable life. It boosts efficiency and productivity as well as improves self-control and discipline as well as boosts confidence and self-esteem as well as promoting wellbeing and satisfaction. Through establishing habits and remaining conscientious when it comes to our behavior and actions and actions, we are able to move toward achieving our goals, and live a happier and more successful life.

The overall goal of this chapter is to give you the tools and techniques you require to establish positive habits and create consistency in your daily life and take steps toward your goals with more efficiency and ease.

Chapter 12: The Role Of Positive Mindset And Attitude

The significance that your attitudes and perspectives play when it comes to executing and reaching your goals. The power of positive thinking and the ways it affects your decisions and behaviours, and we'll go over strategies and strategies you can apply to build an attitude and mindset that is positive.

Mental state and attitude are a part of the manner in which you perceive and approach your goals as well as your life generally. A positive attitude and mindset could help you remain positive, focused and positive, facing difficulties or setbacks. You may be able to tackle your goals in a positive and focused manner and take the necessary steps towards success.

In order to develop a positive mindset and attitude, it's essential to focus on redefining negative thoughts and thoughts, as well as use positive affirmations and appreciation. It is also possible to find excellent role models, as well as surround yourself with positive and positive people.

Being able to maintain a positive mindset and attitude is an essential factor in reaching happiness and living a happy life. Positive attitude refers to an approach to thinking which focuses on the positive regardless of the situation and looks for opportunities as well as solutions instead of dwelling on the difficulties or failures. Positive attitude is the way to approach life with joy and enthusiasm despite the midst of difficulties and failures.

Motivation and determination increase Positive mental and outlook can boost the motivation of people and their determination because it motivates us to focus on the achievements and accomplishments that we've achieved instead of focusing on the setbacks and mistakes. This can help us stay motivated and active both in the workplace and our private lives.

Enhances resilience and improves coping Positive mental and attitude can help build the resilience of our coping skills and resilience because it enables people to recover after difficulties and failures and view them as opportunities to develop and growth.

Improves well-being and happiness: Research has shown that having positive attitudes and a positive mindset could lead to greater health and happiness as it helps us concentrate on what is good about life, and find joy and happiness in our lives.

Improves relationships and communication Positive attitude and mental state can also improve our interactions and our communication as it allows us to interact with people with empathy, compassion and compassion instead of negativity or critique.

The importance of having the importance of a positive attitude and mindset to achieve success and living satisfaction in life is essential. It improves motivation and perseverance improves the ability to cope and persevere improves happiness and well-being as well as improves relationships and communications. If we adopt a positive mindset and outlook, we can achieve our goals and lead a the most fulfilling and successful life.

The overall goal of this chapter is to provide you with the knowledge and techniques you'll need to build a positive attitude and outlook, as well as to move forward towards your goals by generating a sense of optimism and confidence.

Chapter 13: Seeking Support And Accountability

Support and accountability while taking actions towards the goals you have set. This article will examine the many kinds of accountability and support that you can avail as well as explore strategies and tactics you can employ to create networks of accountability and support your daily life.

The importance of accountability and support is one of the primary elements in implementing and reaching your goals. If you are seeking out support from other people You can draw on an abundance of experience as well as experience and motivation in addition to benefiting of the encouragement and accountability you receive from working alongside other people to achieve a common purpose.

There are numerous types of accountability and support you could seek such as mentorship, coaching as well as support groups. All of them can offer you the support and support you need to get started on your objectives.

In order to build a community that is accountable and supportive It is essential to determine your desires and needs, then find the right resources and those who can aid you in reaching your targets. Consider forming your own accountability group, or joining the existing group of people who have identical goals.

Support and accountability from others can play a significant role to achieving success and leading the life you want to live. The support can take the form of support in the form of encouragement and support from your family, friends colleagues, mentors, or coworkers It can also be an invaluable resource in the face of obstacles and failures. The concept of accountability is taking responsibility for your actions, and also being held accountable for the results from those actions. it could be a significant motivation to achieve the goals we set for ourselves. Below are some strategies to get help and accountability could help:

1.Increases motivation and drive Support system: having a supportive network as well as being accountable to other people can boost motivation and resolve, because it helps us feel accountable and encourages to keep on the right track and move towards objectives.

2.Provides the opportunity to draw inspiration and support: Asking for help and direction from other people with similar experiences may provide guidance and inspiration as well as help us deal with setbacks and challenges.

3.Improves self-awareness and self reflection: The obligation to other people can assist in enhancing self-awareness and self reflection, since it helps us reflect on our decisions and the progress we've made as well as to adjust when required.

4.Builds connections as well as a feeling of community. Getting help and accountability from other people helps to create connections and feel a sense of community as it provides opportunities for connecting and cooperation.

It is clear that seeking assistance and accountability is a key aspect of achieving the success you desire and leading a happy life. It boosts motivation and resolve as well as provides encouragement and inspiration, enhances self-awareness, self-reflection, as well as helps build relationships and create feelings of belonging. Through seeking out assistance and accountability from others, we will be able to reach our goals, and enjoy an enjoyable and fulfilling life.

The overall goal of this chapter is to give you the tools and techniques you'll need to get help and accountability when you move toward your objectives, as well as to establish a strong and dependable system of support in your daily life.

Chapter 14: Accepting Failure And Learning From Your Mistakes

The impact of failures and mistakes in the course of taking action and achieving your goals. The course will explore the psychology behind failure, and ways to reframe your perception regarding it. Additionally, we discuss strategies and methods to gain knowledge from mistakes and make them opportunities to grow and develop.

The risk of making mistakes and failing is inevitable elements of your journey to success. It's important to realize that mistakes and failures are normal and a valuable aspect of progress and learning and accept them, rather than let them keep the way.

Reframe the perspective you have on the mistakes and failures you must focus on the development and learning opportunities they offer instead of focusing in the negative elements. It is also possible to seek the advice and assistance of other people, and think about seeking the help of coaches and mentors that can help you make the most of your mistakes and use them to your advantage to develop.

In the end, this chapter will provide you with the knowledge and strategies you require to recognize failure and mistakes as normal and essential aspect of pursuing and achieving your goals. You will also learn to take them as opportunities for improvement and growth.

Chapter 15: Living A Fulfilling Life Via Action

A fulfilled and happy life is making deliberate and thoughtful progress to achieve your dreams and goals. It could mean defining clearly defined goals, and developing a strategy to achieve the goals. It also means striving to achieve those goals every day. This also involves regularly reflecting about and reviewing the priorities you set to ensure the actions you take are in line to your values and the thing that is important to you.

A crucial aspect to living an enjoyable life through action is to identify your passions and the reason for your existence. That could involve exploring many activities and interests to discover your passions and hobbies that give you enjoyment and satisfaction while also discovering your talents and areas in which you could contribute to the world. If you focus on the things that you love and the things you cherish and value, you can find purpose and significance in your choices and life experiences.

Alongside finding your purpose and passion in life, you must be able to create and work towards specific goals. This could involve defining both long and short-term goals that are based on your personal beliefs as well as what matters most for you. Set goals that are clear and achievable could provide guidance and motivation throughout your day, and satisfaction of achieving these goals may give you a feelings of fulfillment.

A key aspect of living the life of a complete person includes taking care of yourself. The process could involve putting in efforts to maintain your physical and mental wellbeing, for example by engaging in regular exercise, eating an adequate diet and ensuring that you get enough sleep. Also, it could mean setting guidelines and scheduling time for personal care activities like things that give enjoyment and relaxation. When you are taking proper care of your self and taking care of yourself, you will be sure that you'll have the motivation and focus to take effective actions towards achieving your goals and goals.

Being a complete person through actions requires identifying your purpose and passion as well as defining and pursuing specific goals, as well as taking care of your health. When you're actively looking for what's the most important to you, and by living in alignment with your ideals and beliefs, you can create an inner sense of importance and significance to your existence and experience the feeling of happiness.

Being able to live a life full of joy is something that a lot of people seek to achieve. This means finding meaning and meaning for one's life as well as pursuing pursuits that bring happiness and satisfaction. The best way to achieve this is to take actions. When we take deliberate and centered steps towards our goals and goals, we could achieve our goals and dreams towards fulfillment, and lead happier lives..

There are many methods that can help you help you live a more fulfilling life:

1.Setting goals and pursuing them Set goals help us concentrate our energies and effort on what's essential for us. This gives us an understanding of our purpose and direction. It also allows us to experience an accomplishment and growth as we work toward achieving goals.

2.Taking proper care of our mental, physical and emotional health By engaging in actions that help us maintain our general well-being including fitness, healthy eating and self-care can allow you feel more energetic in our lives, centered, and resilient.

3. Maintaining and building meaningful relationships Relationships with your relatives, friends and family members can provide happiness, comfort and a sense belonging. If we are actively seeking out these relationships and enhancing them, we are able to enhance our lives and feel at one with others.

4.Making an impact on the world. We can discover meaning and satisfaction when we contribute to something greater than us, like an issue we're committed to or a society that is in need. When we are able to take the initiative in a positive way and find meaning and satisfaction within our lives.

A fulfilled life via action requires creating and meeting goals and looking after our health and relationships and bringing positive change on the planet. If we are actively seeking these goals you can lead an enjoyable and meaningful life.

Chapter 16: Why Should You Trust This Book To Change Your Life?

It's not going to be a secret to you that at one point in my life I was not the most productive person I've ever known. I had to endure a lot of uncomfortable "what are you doing with your life?" discussions in family dinners and were never done asking questions and provoking me. Every time I was with my family I was a victim of those who asked me about what I was doing in my life. Since I didn't have anything to show pride in or even a passion about. In the grand scheme of things I think they're just showing an interest in me and showing concern for my. However, because I was feeling bad about myself, this was obvious to everyone else. In the course of a couple of years, I reached that point where that my head was about to explode because my parents kept in asking me to take actions.

To make me feel more comfortable, I chose to take action.

In all honesty I would imagine that questions and pushes is a bit annoying to me, and even demotivating since "I could do it myself at the time I wanted it!" But, in the in your heart, receiving assistance and push from others can be a pleasant experience. It is as you read this book to solve your questions, inspire you and push you to take action! The book helped me understand that, not only did I did not have anything particularly exciting happening in my life, but I also had people seeking to encourage me to take taking action, because they are proud of them and wish they will have the best outcome for me. I started to feel ashamed of not acting due to the feeling that I had let them down.

I realized that I must alter my life as deep down I wanted to be accomplished in my career. I had to quit doing nothing, and wasting my time in the sofa to make something tangible happen in my life. This wasn't simply to ensure that I could have something interesting to discuss at social gatherings and dinners neither. It was something I needed to accomplish for myself, since I was bored of my boring existence I'd created for myself, and was meticulously maintaining through practicing my couch potato abilities as if I was preparing to compete in the Olympics.

I began putting all my energy and energy into researching and eating everything with the potential to improve my life. I listened to TED Talks and YouTube videos, read audiobooks, and even bought books that allowed me to write my notes on the margins. Researching for weeks transformed into months and after that, years. gradually I began to make huge progress towards making a difference in my life. An enticing sentence here, and an encouraging pep talk later was enough to motivate me to make a an impact on my life. And I'd go on to do it. After that, I'd make a second one, and another. In no time, I was making huge changes within my own life.

After having read books that were incredibly inspirational such as The 10X Rule by Grant Cardone as well as Consider and Grow Rich by Napoleon Hill, as well as Getting Things Done by David Allen and I was so inspired, I decided to share my personal experiences and knowledge into a book for other also to enjoy. This is why I opened an excel spreadsheet, and now I'm writing this inspiring book to assist you in changing your lifestyle.

When I witness people who are spending their time doing nothing particularly now that I see how simple to stop this cycle of waste, I become extremely frustrated. I know that this occurs because you're not aware of the best way to end the cycle, or you are aware of the process, but the process of implementing this knowledge is to be a daunting task. There is an apparent gap in many instances that connects knowledge with execution. This missing link means that even though it's simple to acquire understanding and rationally comprehend why the logic of reasoning is crucial and must be followed however, it's often difficult to put it into practice. There are few sources that acknowledge the processes of mind and cycle that an average individual must go through to free themselves from the limitations that hinder individuals from attaining the goals they would like to achieve in life. Yes, I am aware.

I can remember spending the majority of my time moving back and forth applying new techniques like an expert for a few days only to slip back to old habits and never achieve the great outcomes I began tapping into. Every time, I'd make a change and appear to be a completely different man for a couple of days, only to return to the couch potato self which I was so afraid of. Each moment that this took place that it was more difficult to let go from the couch potato habit and then finally make progress that was lasting. As if, each time I failed I was determined to try again, believing that failing was inevitable, so I gave myself every chance to relapse back into my routines. So, another bad habit began to emerge, where I allowed myself enough permission to give up and then revert back to my old ways.

I'm sure I'm not the only one who experiences this and I'm sure you are too. Around the globe there are hundreds thousands of people committed to their own improvement, however, they struggle tremendously in taking what they've learned into practice. Some may see incredible result for just a few days, weeks and even months. Yet, it is a slow slide back into the same old pattern that appears to be inevitable each time. The worst part is that they're brilliant possessing a vast amount of information that will change their lives but they don't have knowledge of how to use that information consistently in a way that can change their lives.

If you're in the same boat is the case, then you're exactly the person you wrote the novel to. I wrote this book to the people you know, including your friends you have with your family and friends, and everyone else you know who's become accustomed to seeking change but finding it difficult to begin or keep going with the changes you decide to make. This book was written for those who are willing to put aside the discussion of their goals and begin doing what they've always wanted to do. The book will help you break out of the cycle of talking, wishing or wishing and becoming embarrassed that nothing happens to allow you to begin seeing the physical realisation of everything that you've always dreamed of to your life.

This is from my deepest heart. I am convinced that you or anyone else who has read this article is bound to be a success. I believe that this is since you could not constantly set out to discover more, make those connections and complete the missing parts if you weren't completely committed to living your life to one of the most fulfilling you can be able to make it. Karma could be called it what you want You could refer to it as fate, or refer to it as fate. You can really use whatever name you wish. I'll call it your decision to do something about it and see outcomes.

If you're willing to be willing to live your dream life that you've wanted to live and in all ways you can, that's what we'll accomplish with you. Learn how you can not just reach your goals but also make your life reflect your relationships, interests and career choices, as well as the wealth, health, religion and all the other things you really want to see within your own life. If you learn everything I've taught you, there is anything you are unable to do and integrate in your lifestyle. From now on everything else you'll learn will be easy to put into practice because you'll be armed with the right piece of information, and you'll know precisely what you can do to harness the human nature of your being to attain the kind of progress you want in your own life.

Another key that I'd like to share with you prior to the beginning of this work, and that crucial element is a particular way of thinking that I am convinced all people should be working towards understanding the importance of integrating, nurturing, and fostering within their own lives. The key to this is the importance in valuing your self, and taking note of the beauty in the world around you. You're made from identical materials and substance as every person that you dream of becoming, or would like to be. Everyone who came before you who has accomplished the goals you desire is composed from the same materials that you are, and has the same capabilities and abilities that you have. It means that you are able to use the same abilities and skills like they do. It is not something that differentiates you from them, other than the fact they've learned to be proud of themselves and cooperate to themselves at an extent that they're not prepared to achieve within their own lives. This isn't a quality earned by luck or because they were unique neither. This is a value that they created in their own minds by deciding to believe that they were worth and deserving of all the things they desired as everyone could be, so they had no excuse why they couldn't also enjoy and achieve anything they wanted in their lives.

If you start to appreciate your self to the highest level you can, and appreciate your ability to be creative and be anything you wish to have in your life, wonderful events begin to happen within your own life. Opportunities arise from seemingly fantastical places, opening possibilities for you to fulfill all the dreams that you've had all your entire life. The world around you begins to appreciate you more also, when they see that you've recognized the value of yourself and you'll receive no more than you're worth. People suddenly would like to show the best you have to offer. They are more generous with you as they reward your more generously and allow you to accomplish the tasks you'd like to do since they are confident in you because they have learned that you are a trustworthy person.

If you're looking to unleash the magic of your life and begin to take advantage of every chance that's yours, the first step is to recognize the value of your self and appreciate you more than others could ever appreciate yourself. It may feel awkward initially, but it isn't always easy to do so particularly in a society that teaches us to not value ourselves, and in which we are often taught that being too self-centered is bad however it's one of the most significant choices you'll ever make to your self. Through this particular book, you will discover many great strategies for yourself to recognize the value of yourself in every possible way to naturally draw new opportunities to your life. In this way, you'll be able to realize the extent of the real magic of an experience that can change your life.

Answer These Questions...

1. Have you taken any steps that you have implemented, even the most insignificant item you are happy about, in order to begin altering your lifestyle? If so, what has they done to benefit you?

2. How do you let you to apply the information you've learned and all you have learned, more effectively?

3. Do you have at least 10 things you appreciate in yourself today?

4. Are you willing to begin the journey of your desires?

Chapter 17: You Know You Want Better For Yourself

I'm sure that you're looking through Take Action because you are eager to transform your lifestyle. It's been a long daydreaming about what you want to achieve and working hard to change your life, while experiencing the same slow "initiation period" that most of us have to go through in order to start making real change in our lives. The time has come for you to get past the initial phase that's full of excessive research, but insufficient action. It is time to get into the stage that you start to notice the real change in your life.

Let me tell to let you know prior to proceeding You're already a success. It's not something to make you feel more confident on yourself. It's true. You do your research, you search at real methods to make the change you want, and are determined to keep trying until you discover all the information you require for making those real-life changes that you desire and want to make in your daily life. They are exactly the characteristics of an effective person which you already have. You already are an accomplished person.

Let me tell the world something today that I would like someone to have advised me earlier on during my self-improvement journey. If you're a novice on your journey, you might think that you're not satisfied until you have reached the point that you've received your prize and achieved the goal of what you in mind to accomplish. If you're aiming to purchase a house and you want to move, for instance, it is possible that you won't feel like you are successful until you have actually bought the house you want. However, this isn't the way success operates. If you opt to think of success in this manner it is actually making yourself vulnerable to failure due to being focused too much on what will happen but not knowing what it is that success really means.

It's all about the final game However, it's not just about the results that you make throughout the process. If you can take the time to recognize the powerful actions that you have taken to achieve the goal as a aspect of your success it will be clear that you're already at the point of reaching your goals which means you have already achieved success. As an example, purchasing this book and agreeing to reading it an enormous step in the direction of achievement because it brings you closer to the achievement of your personal goal. In the absence of this process of collecting information and learning in the process, you may not possess enough knowledge required to take the actions which will bring about the results you want. This is really a major step to your accomplishment which is why I'd like to say congratulations!

Once you understand that every step that you take towards your achievement is, as a whole an act of success, you see that you're already on the right track to success. A simple change in view of the world means that in the future you will no longer be able to claim that you're not yet successful "yet" or that you "are not making enough progress" because you're already taking huge strides. Each step which brings you towards your goal is a success and it means you're already a success.

I'm willing to wager that you've considered give up on this adventure at the very least or even more than once prior to. Perhaps you have taken breaks when you decided to stop investing in the process because you believed that you were not producing any results, so you didn't think it was worth the effort then you find yourself at it again. In spite of the many times you thought of quitting or take breaks that you might have had to take however, you're still increasing your chances of success. This is a hugely impressive achievement. You've taken the first step or next step which is definitely worth celebration and congratulations!

To get to creating success in your life, and getting closer to your goal is more than fretting about how much you dislike your current situation, or the amount of shame or discontent you may find yourself feeling about the place you're currently. Your journey to where you are today has nothing to do with be about removing yourself from being the person you believe you've been all is about bringing you closer to the achievement that you are designed to achieve. The time has come for you to acknowledge that and start to think of yourself as an accomplished person. There's nothing to feel embarrassed or ashamed of or ashamed of, and there's no excuse to be held responsible to decisions that you taken during the past. All of these choices will can lead to you right now today making the decision to alter your life to the best of your abilities. Your life is already one step closer to reaching your goal simply for having made this decision. Let me prove this to you!

Many of the most popular persons who later became well-known names began with enormous mistakes. Steve Jobs and Steve Wozniak who were the founding fathers of Apple among others had a number of mistakes ranging from constructing poorly operating devices and computers, in search of investors prior to the time that Apple began to take off. Many people told Jeff Bezos that Amazon would not succeed, but nevertheless, it did. The entrepreneur behind IKEA, Ingvar Kamprad, was similarly told however, IKEA is an internationally renowned for its furniture and lifestyle brands today. Many people across the world of business, sports industries, as well as smaller areas of society were told numerous times that their goals could not be achieved or were not worthwhile, but they got their hands on it. They continued to try and tried again regardless of the number of attempts they made, but ultimately some of their attempts stood out and they were able to see that they had succeeded to achieve the outcomes they wanted.

The only true failure could ever happen throughout your life is when you give up completely and will never attempt to do it again. If you choose to do this, and you continue doing it for the rest of your existence, perhaps you could consider it as a success. If you continue to search for solutions and do everything you can to figure out ways to overcome, whatever you've been calling an failure really is the result of an obstacle. This is simply you figuring out ways to overcome the obstruction. The process of overcoming difficulties and navigating to overcome them, is a fundamental part of the journey to achieving happiness throughout your life. You are now in the process of achieving success.

While we are launching to embark on this adventure together I'd like to ask you to perform one last task to me. Do you have the ability to do this? It is my wish that you recognize the power and singularity you truly are, as well as the unique and special desires and goals have been for you. It is my wish that you realize that nobody else in the world can ever have or desires the same things you do or desire or desires, and no one other person will be able to fully grasp the goals you're aiming to accomplish in your own life. In addition, due to your uniqueness and the uniqueness of your goals are, there's no way to compare your path with anyone else's. There is no one else who has any idea about what you'll need to do to get the place you'd like to be, except for the person who is you. This is why there's absolutely nothing to suggest that you're an unavoidable success, since the way I'm sitting this moment, it appears that you're a certain successful, and that the ultimate goal is much further away than you believe. I'll bet somehow regardless of it being only a tiny part of it for the moment, you be sure that I'm right, and that it will be the same until you achieve the outcomes you want.

You're a truly amazing, unique person which is why I am thrilled to provide you with tools that will assist you in recognizing your distinctiveness as well as help you achieve the goals you have set in your life. The journey ahead will be a blast, and I look at being there to assist you along your journey. I want to thank you again for inviting me to join you and trusting me to be the one to assist you take off from your sofa and to live the life you've always wanted.

Answer These Questions...

1. You can describe yourself using a style that represents you the best.

2. Which of your own qualities do you look forward to learning more about in this adventure?

3. What obstacles do you personally face and are trying to conquer as you go through this book?

4. With your own words, redefine your own perceived mistakes so you are able to see these as an element of the journey which has led you to this point and to the next stage of development in your life.

5. Develop a mantra that can aid you in overcoming every obstacle that you encounter throughout your life, so you are motivated to continue your journey whenever when you encounter difficulties, no matter if they are physical, mental or even psychological.

Chapter 18: What Are You Going To Do About It?

After every individual chapter and in the course of the book, you'll be asked take a survey that will assist to shift from an inactive mindset to an active one. Did you have success in doing this in two chapters? Yes? You are doing something and that's great! It is important to keep making progress, today in order to keep achieving the best output from all you've been doing to improve your knowledge.

"Be the bull at everything you do in life" Tilman Fertitta - Tilman Fertitta

While reading particularly a novel that is long It is easy to be absorbed in a passive way everything you're going through. While you might end up understanding the content but you might struggle to break out of this inactive mindset to a habit of thinking critically about the content and how you can incorporate it in your own everyday life. It is essential to get out of the habit of being passive in order to apply what you've discovered. Be sure to never forget these questions and you make sure to answer them with a clear and thoughtful manner, so you make the most of the answers.

Make sure to keep notes on your phone, as well as in your notebook can be kept on hand while you're reading the book. So, if you are reading something that you feel is significant or something you want to recall, you'll be able to note it immediately! Once you've written things down and keep them in mind, they'll stick deeper into your brain.

Answer These Questions…

1. Why did you decide to buy this book first?

2. What issue are you looking to resolve by the book?

3. You've already done many hours into transforming your lifestyle, so you've likely already conducted some research for yourself. What can you do to maintain an open mind and continue to keep reading until you've completed your book then continue reading? (Note to approach everything with a wide-open mind regardless of how well you think you understand about the topic is the most effective way to absorb all that you're reading. This results in higher degrees of improvement.)

4. What special endgame(s) and/or goal(s) are you working towards in mind for yourself that you wish to reach?

5. Define your ideal way of life. Take a look at all eight main areas in your life. These include your wealth, health careers, relationships, your love life, your relationship with your self, interests, and your faith.

Chapter 19: Changing The Mindset
of of Couch Potato

Are you going through self-improvement materials, picking the parts that are relevant to you as well as which ones do not apply to you? Don't do that. As you read through this book, I'd like readers to understand that every part of this book can be applied to you. This book is applicable to you since I put it together with you in your mind. I wrote it with the knowledge that you've already gotten yourself educated about self-improvement issues, as well as having attempted to incorporate some of these strategies in your daily lifestyle. This book was written for people who know that they may have tried a few of these ideas and follow them however, the vast most of the things you've discovered you're either applying in a haphazard manner, or fail to do so. Although you may want to put them into practice even if you think they should be implemented however, you're not. It's a struggle, but you are determined to do so, yet you've yet to. You even realize that if you implemented the changes you want to make, you'd have a head start, yet you've not incorporated these changes.

It is the fact that you've not yet implemented these ideas, or did not implement them in the way you would like to might suggest that you have to read this publication as if didn't know that the content existed. If you are studying something and think, "yeah, I already know that" in your head, pull yourself back and deliberately put that thought aside. Reframe your thoughts towards "hmm, interesting!" And continue to read as if everything in this book is completely unfamiliar to you. Just this one thing can enable you to take in and make use of more from this text than you've never done before. This implies that you will stop learning and begin to do. This, naturally is the place where changes in your life come from.

Now, irrespective whether that you've accumulated, or not, you're immersed in the status quo of a couch potato. Your life is full of sitting, inactive, doing little, trying to justify what you've accomplished that's not significant yet. It is easy to accumulate dreams saying to yourself that you'll be successful one day, but you're not doing anything important to move closer to making those goals the reality of your life. At times, you might consider taking actions, and you may fill your day in with activities that cause you to feel overwhelmed instead of spending your time doing activities that assist you to achieve your goals. You could, for instance, create a strategy and make it more refined several times instead of creating plans and begin making real progress to see your plan come to fruition. At this point you may be saying to yourself that you won't be able to begin until the xyz event occurs, or that you'll not achieve any substantial progress this morning and you may be better off waiting for an opportunity to have a better day and more prospects. There is a chance that you are convinced it is impossible that you can do any worthwhile thing this day, and you may decide to let some projects accumulate before getting underway so that once you have the motivation, you're making a difference by the energy. You could even have been telling yourself a variety of different things for yourself to believe you're accomplishing enough or there's nothing you can accomplish at the moment to help you get the direction you'd like to take. There's a chance that you're not deliberately doing this You may not be aware you're doing it however, you're doing it.

One of the most difficult aspects of being caught in the cycle of not taking actions is when you enter into a vicious cycle of shame that causes you to take action more difficult as time passes. The particular shame cycle that you'll be entering will see you making excuses as to the reasons you aren't able to start today, then being embarrassed that you did been putting off getting begun. Perhaps, you feel ashamed because instead of making a decision that was productive you were sat in a corner doing nothing.

Recognize that throughout your life, there is many different ends. It is possible that you have your primary objective to reach an attainable wealth goal or skill level such as, for instance, but it's not your only goal you're striving for. There is also the same endgames in your relationships, your interests, in well-being, as well as in different areas in your life which are equally important as the one you're now concentrating upon. In this regard, there's always something that you could be working towards your goal of living the life you've always wanted however there's no way to work to help in a particular aspect in creating the life that you'd like to live. If, for instance, you're focused on the launch of your business, however you are unable to take more action right now it is possible to spend some making time for the people that matter to you within your own life or even learning a new skill in the hobbies you enjoy. These sorts of things will be more effective as opposed to sitting in a solitary position as they help to develop the fundamental mindset of getting moving and creating momentum within your own life. They allow you to create greater success for yourself as you start to build an habit of inventing and utilizing momentum to reach your goals in all fields that you live in.

Your mental outlook is a effective tool in your daily life. It's got the potential to allow you to attain almost anything you wish to. A lot of people are unaware the extent to which their mental state goes beyond than the one is centered around the particular subject they're considering right now. Your mental state includes the way you think regarding specific subjects, in addition to the underlying mindset which is behind each topic and gives you an organized framework to guide what you'll be and think in various scenarios. Through the use of individual scenarios to develop your mentality to help you discover how to take actions, create strategies, build momentum using this momentum to realize your dreams and goals throughout the process to the desired goal. In this way then, you will concentrate on developing your mentality around the personal final goal that made you purchase this book and the framework that guides your thoughts about everything you want to accomplish in your everyday life.

Five fundamental mental techniques you have apply to build your mental picture in relation to your own personal goal, and also around the overall framework. They include practicing mindfulness, using auto-suggestion's power, setting boundaries to yourself, giving yourself the freedom to dream and putting your faith in yourself.

Cultivating Mindfulness

Mindfulness is not an enticing or passive activity that allows people to fall into a state of the state of meditation or deep levels of tranquility at the touch of a button. It is an dynamic and active practice that allows you to observe your emotions, your mental, and physical experiences at any time to be more aware and gain awareness of what you're doing. If you are looking to do any thing in your life, such as altering your behavior and reaching the goals you have set, being mindful may aid you in understanding what is holding your back, so you are able to begin moving towards the obstacles.

One of the easiest ways to comprehend mindfulness is to relate the experience of mindfulness to watching information from the world around you, however instead, you're watching things inside the world. When you are outside it is a matter of using the five senses that you have to perceive what's happening in the world around you as well as to understand your experiences you're experiencing. Inside it is your ability to slow down and examine your feelings, thoughts and bodily responses to your surroundings to provide a greater comprehension of what you feel and experience in every moment.

Knowing what's happening in your personal the world can be a fantastic way to gain insight into what makes it difficult to complete specific things. You can also discover how you can maximize your strengths in addition to minimizing your inherent weak points, and help manage the different scenarios you're in. Use this knowledge to improve your performance in issues, and to assist you in learning how to maintain a healthier lifestyle in order to lessen stress or ease it as well as to help yourself by assisting you in many other ways. In reality, the knowledge that you get from actively watching the inner workings of you can alter the way you live your life, in ways that you could never think of.

To build a sense consciousness, and the capacity to manage your thoughts through the practice of mindfulness, start asking yourself three questions. These three inquiries can be answered at any moment throughout the day and over time, will become an integral aspect of your day to daily experience. Three questions to be asking are "How am I feeling right now?" "What am I thinking right now?" as well as "What do I want or need right now?" The answers to the three questions above will aid you in understanding the current state of affairs and help you to handle it efficient and effectively. It is important to ask these types of questions any time you observe changes in your thinking and emotions, or even your physical appearance, especially in the event that you're not happy with the way you're experiencing. They can be used when you realize that you are engaging with unproductive behaviors like using excuses to sit around instead of engaging in actions.

It is also possible to achieve mindfulness through allowing yourself ample moments to relax and learn to understand you more deeply. Examining your diverse ideas, feelings physical and mental sensations as well as what they are feeling inside the person you are is a wonderful way to get conscious of how life is as it is from the point of view you have. Being aware of yourself in those quiet times can help you comprehend who you are and the reason you're in this way. This can go a long way in helping you to comprehend yourself in events that are happening ahead of you. So, instead of being caught up in a sea of thoughts during these scenarios, you'll be able to accurately and rapidly discern your thoughts, emotions and feelings, and discover sensible ways to assist you in navigating the scenario.

If you're ready to start taking action towards meditation, here are three fantastic activities to do in the present. These activities should be practiced daily to ensure that when you are going about your day, you're constantly enhancing your ability to be mindful and helping yourself improve your self-starting skills.

One of the first things you could attempt right now is an exercise that is 5:7 in duration. This easy exercise will take no less than 60 second and can to bring you back to your body, so it is possible to concentrate on the experience you're experiencing here today. You aren't obliged to limit yourself to only 60 seconds. You are able to certainly spend as long as you'd like this workout! In order to start your 5:7 breathing move your spine straight and hold one hand in front of your stomach. After that, inhale by letting your nose breathe slowly to count five. Do this for two seconds and breathe out by mouth until you reach 7 counts. Do this for 2 minutes before inhaling by letting your nose in to count five then starting the procedure over. If you can do this for only 5-10 minutes can assist in bringing your attention back to the present in order to embrace the world from a place of awareness, and not an interruption.

The 5,4 3, 2 1 practice of mindfulness is an excellent one for you to explore also. The particular method is a great way to engage the senses of all five It is an excellent technique to get back to your present whenever you feel disoriented or lost in thought. It is a great practice to use when you find yourself putting off tasks or just wasting your time. it helps you to ground yourself, and help you get back in contact with the things that you truly want from your the world! Start with a look around your room and noting 5 things that you notice. Imagine them in your mind using phrases like "I see a yellow car; I see a purple vase, I see pink flowers," and the list goes on. Next, you'll need to look for four things which you are able to touch. Find objects that are close to your hand, and possess different textures. Remind yourself with the words "I feel the rough texture of my jeans" or "I feel the soft texture of this couch" and the like. You should then identify 3 sounds you hear. Then, explain what you heard to yourself. Find two items you are able to smell. Then, talk about the smell with yourself. If it is necessary stand up, search for something you can smell like flowers or a candle as it is important to activate the senses during this exercise. Then, find something you smell. It might be the lingering taste of the meal you consumed, or it could be the result of a chew gum or have one sip of water to give a different flavor you to identify. After you've mastered every one of your five senses, you can affirm your objective to yourself, so that you can keep it at the top of your head, and begin to work towards achieving your target!

Another excellent way you can utilize to swiftly bring yourself in the present moment to describe your experience before you. It is common to get within our minds thinking about numerous things, or worrying about the things we have to accomplish which can cause the process of getting started more difficult. In this case think from the point of being aware that you're getting up to perform, which can help get you prepared to take action. You could, for instance, use the phrase: "It is Friday, and I've had an amazing working day, but the moment I returned to my home, I sat on my couch. Then, I'm rising to meet my goals and accomplish amazing things throughout the remainder of my life!" This type of self-talking will keep you focused and present in your life. It will also help inspire you to get serious about achieving the goals you have set!

Leveraging the Power of Auto-Suggestion

Auto-suggestion is one of the forms of habitual thinking which everyone is exposed to. Auto-suggestions arise from your mind thinking about the same things frequently enough that your brain thinks of regardless of whether you've no intention of creating the thought you are thinking about. Once this occurs then you're actually experiencing auto-suggestion within your mind. If the auto-suggestions you receive were not designed by you, you may be surprised to discover they're filled with negative thoughts which make you feel like you're not able to accomplish what you'd like to do. As an example, any of your excuses to you are likely the result of the auto-suggestions you're currently receiving.

Making your auto-suggestions work for you rather than limit you, offers you an opportunity to develop auto-generated thoughts that motivate your actions to make you more likely to be able to actually complete your tasks. Five great methods to begin taking control of the suggestions of your autopilot in order utilize them in your favor. The five methods include developing a personal diet by using affirmations, using repetition to your advantage using visualization, and utilizing the alpha state of your mind.

A diet for the mind is the most effective way to begin your process of changing the auto-suggestions you receive. The true meaning of a mental diet can be accomplished by eliminating all thoughts and conversations that doesn't contribute towards achieving the outcome that you wish to see in the world. In the case of, say, if you tend to talk about yourself in negative terms which causes you to feel as if you're unworthy of, unworthy, or not worthy to have what you want You must cut the behavior. This can be done by listening to the self-talk you engage in and at any time you see your negative self-talk surfacing you should be consciously eliminating and erasing the thoughts. Within your head, you need to say "DELETE, ERASE!" whenever you notice yourself getting caught up with your self-talk. Doing it disrupts your thinking process and allows the mind to shift the things you're thinking about. When you've deleted or erased that thoughts, you are able to shift your focus to positively and positive. In the context of the scenario your currently in, you may consider using mental instructions to direct your focus and thoughts in particular if you're facing a difficult circumstance. There is a tendency to struggle in the midst of a lot of negativity in your mind when you're in stressful situations and directing your thoughts with things such as "calm down," "focus," or "slow down," will assist you in taking control of your mind as well. It is recommended to practice the mental diet for at least 30 days but you'll need to practice this for longer, since it can transform the way that you utilize your brain throughout various circumstances.

Affirmations can be described as an affirming statements that you can make to yourself especially those who are seeking a boost. Your affirmation must be spoken with a positive, current third person, tense statement which helps you changing the story within your head. They can be spoken in a moment and can also be something you decide to say to yourself repeatedly over and again when you discover you navigating patterns of behavior that you wish to let go of. An excellent example of affirmations is "I accomplish anything I desire" or "I take the first step." If affirming yourself seem a bit strange Consider researching some which are pertinent to your particular behavior and objectives, and then write the affirmations down so you are able to refer back to the list whenever you're looking for an affirmation. When you notice you are engaging in a negative auto-suggestive, you can refer to your list of affirmations to start reaffirming different thoughts you have to your self. In time, the other ideas are going to replace the auto-suggestions you receive, and will prove to be better than those that you're currently dealing with.

Repetition is vital in the creation of auto-suggestions because auto-suggestions form habitual and are developed by repetition. To maximize the effectiveness of repetition when you are creating auto-suggestions, it is best need to choose the thing you'll need to repeatedly repeat to incorporate into your routine thought patterns. A mantra, affirmation or even a brand new thought is a good idea to contemplate in this regard, since it can offer you the most effective opportunity to keep repeating the exact same phrase repeatedly in your mind, becoming an auto-suggestive. The phrase you choose to repeat or words ought to be something is repeated when you think you should, whenever you can remember, as well as every throughout the day! Also it is not necessary that you have to engage in negative or demotivating thoughts in order to consider the phrases you repeat. You can simply consider the phrases whenever you are able to strengthen them, and then turn your thoughts into automatic suggestions. Create a routine of repeating the words. In this way you'll make your brain an habit of saying the task without effort. That's the way you'd like it to be! Keep a notebook, modern notes in your smartphone, and set a timer in your day when you write down those phrases that you've chosen repeatedly in order to create them in your brain every day on a daily basis.

Visualization is another instrument that can be used to increase the effectiveness of auto-suggestions. As per the many research projects conducted, including the impact of mental training in the development of a particular motor skill, conducted by Clark, L. Verdelle[1Your body and mind aren't aware of the distinction between the real world and your imagination. When you shut your eyes and think about doing things, the mental practice can trigger similar mental images which actually participating in the activity would produce. Imagine yourself completing everything and getting it all done and then feeling happy over it is an excellent solution to resolving your auto-suggestions. Imagine what you wish to happen, for instance your getting up off the couch, taking action that is successful, and not the things you are afraid of happening like lying on your couch throughout your life, in a constant lack of action. Do minimum of 10 minutes of consciously desired visualization each day in order to develop fresh auto-suggestions. Also, you can remember these visualizations at anytime you're experiencing feelings of being dismotivated, or depressed since this could aid in building the courage to rise up and step involved, not rest in a state of demotivation and unmotivated.

Also, you must focus on achieving an Alpha state of mind for you be able to bring about powerful shifts in the auto-suggestions you make. A state of mind that is alpha implies that you slow your mind and do things consciously instead of leaving it all in the hands of your mind's subconscious. In order to work on your brain's ability to change the processes that are taking place within your mind's subconscious, taking control of your actions can be a fantastic approach to understand what's happening inside your brain and alter the way it operates.

Mindfulness is the strongest way to reach the state of alpha because it allows you to integrate the awareness of your mind into all that you do. So, rather than being able to feed your mind's subconscious your self-limiting habits that hinder your progress You can break through these patterns to propel yourself into a state of freedom that allows you to be who you are. In order to achieve this kind of meditation, you're likely to need to block the time needed for mindfulness, so you'll need choose a time and location that you'll not be disoriented. It is important to not focus only on being in the state of alpha and building the courage that you require to keep the self-limiting habits you have created.

When you've taken the time and you are ready to settle in a quiet place and let yourself sink into a deep meditative state. It is possible to do this by using your mindfulness 5:7 breathing practice, by doing this exercise repeatedly over for a few minutes. When you keep doing this, you'll feel more at ease and more in the present in the present moment. At this point it is possible to notice the self-limiting habits you might experience that could be restricting you. Perhaps, for instance, you have a pattern is to convince yourself that you are not taking actions that are beneficial for your health and helps you achieve your objectives. The goal here is to engage your mind to the patterns to be able to see what it doesn't serve your needs, then it is time to begin breaking your pattern and replace it with something else. It's as if you take control of your mind in general with the statement, "I acknowledge that I am a victim of a habit of arguing myself into engaging in activities that are beneficial for me and it is a self-limiting habit. This is a pattern that I follow as it's much easier to convince myself of things as opposed to getting up and start doing these things. I'm removing this habit as it has been hindering me and I'm not comfortable anymore since I am constantly struggling to make progress in my daily life. For the next few months I'm going to convince myself to do those things that are beneficial for me. I'm going to utilize my thoughts to inspire me to act. The way I use my mind is to help me succeed instead of fighting against that success." This kind of internal dialogue allows you to access all your unconscious patterns and start to change the old ones to ensure that you're free of being stopped from these habits. Once you have awoken from your meditation, it is important to be committed to following your new thought pattern that you presented during the meditation, so you can teach your brain's subconscious to believe on you and your judgement. This is when you begin seeing yourself have more control of your mind and an even greater capacity to break down habits that aren't serving you well to allow you to substitute those that work with the right ones. In time you will find you having the absolute control over your mind and making it simpler to achieve anything you wish to accomplish.

"He who controls his own mind, controls his own destiny." -- Ernest Holmes

Set Limits for Yourself the Surprising Way

Gaining control of your thoughts and using it to benefit yourself comes in an element of encouraging yourself, by giving yourself positive feedback and also from having boundaries set for yourself, and sticking to them regardless of what. Many people who find themselves doing nothing and failing to achieve their objectives often end up stuck in this position due to the fact that they do not establish boundaries for themselves that could otherwise stop the occurrence of such behaviour. Setting boundaries for yourself and to maintain the boundaries you set is crucial as it will aid you in the process of to creating and maintaining limits with others, as well. This, in turn can go far in helping to mentally prepare yourself to be successful in making decisions and making things happen within your daily life.

The very first limit or limits you should establish to your self. It is important to establish the limits of how long you're willing to spend in a corner doing nothing, and the number of excuses you're ready to hear from yourself until you determine that you have had enough. While it may appear ideal to set these limits rigidly and allow your self a small amount of room to move your feet at a level that's right, however there's some formula that you can use to establish limitations for yourself from the beginning, which is essential to get you moving. The most effective way to begin creating limitations on yourself is to start with setting limits that will be easily attainable for you to look through. If, for instance, you realize that after you return after work, you want to take a break before getting things done, set the goal that you'll not be able to relax following work or even be able to rest for 5 minutes, which is a great limitation! Start by allowing yourself 30 to 45 minutes to chill upon returning home. and then decide on a time limit since this will be incredible in comparison to the time spent five hours! Would you like to "relax" less than 30-45 minutes? If so, do so. You can say to you "well then, I'll just relax that half hour tomorrow" Then in the morning you must take action as well! The same way! Choose the level that you can live with in the longer term and move towards the limit. Once you have reached it, keep trying to keep the limit. If you discover it difficult to not want to do things, you can give yourself the option to make use of a set amount of "excuse days" per month. In the example above, perhaps during the month, you get four excuses days that's four days in a month during which you could abstain from doing anything. On the other days of in the same month, you'll be taking steps. In time, you may decrease that time to excused hours instead of excuse days. Find out what is best for you and try to aim at a level that's likely to provide you with what you require, not an approach that will be a hit in other people's book. Keep in mind that you're trying to create a unique ending which nobody else knows about, so If giving yourself ample relaxation and time with your hobbies is what makes you the most productive over the long term, make sure you do it. However, if you're giving yourself too lots of time to relax that you're in no way productive You aren't finding the right equilibrium. Also, if you do not allow yourself to rest even though you know how much you'll need it, then you'll never be able to maintain habit because they don't recognize or respect your individual preferences and needs.

In relation to other people, you have to establish limits on how you will engage about the hopes you've got for yourself. Particularly when dealing with individuals who may not be positive or supportive of your goals Limits are essential. Do not be a passive observer listening to others say that the thing you'd like to achieve is not possible for you to achieve and that you're not able to achieve your wishes due to past performances. Being able to listen to others attempt to disengage you or demotivate yourself isn't something that you have to endure and therefore having some limits is crucial. Set these boundaries by not having a conversations about your goals or desires with people that aren't encouraging and also not believing anything others say about your dreams or capability. In this way, you're refusing to be influenced by anyone else's views about you and your goals, but instead, you're making your own decisions about the thoughts you make.

The ability to maintain your boundaries and limits in yourself as well as in your relationships with others requires time and practice. I suggest that you be reminded of your boundaries, specifically in your actions and thoughts as well as around the thoughts of others and actions each day for minimum 30 days, so that they're still fresh in your memory. In this way, whenever you witness the boundaries of your boundary being violated either by you or someone else and you are able to immediately enforce the boundaries. Then, they will become aspect of your daily life and it'll become simple to recall the boundaries and claim them whenever required.

Give Yourself Permission to Dream

In a unoccupied state during any period of duration can cause it to appear that creating plans and dreams for your future is almost impossible. It is possible that you are thinking about all the things that people have spoken about your goals or you personally in general, and then letting yourself be convinced that it's not feasible for you to realize your goals. It is possible that you have been trying to stop yourself from making an effort to create the dream of your own as you believed that you weren't capable of achieving the dream you had in mind, or thought there was no reason to think about it since it was impossible to believe that to achieve it. However, whatever you've told yourself all along it is important to take the initiative to get away from that belief and shift to a way of thinking where you are able to let yourself dream.

You've probably had the pleasure of hearing a uplifting motivational speech or two on how important it is to dream, as well as about having the freedom to imagine whatever you would like in your the world, and also to believe that it is achievable for you. Let me remind you that I said that I'd aid you in closing this gap, and it is exactly the thing we'll take on.

The length of time that you've been waiting around for or the length of time you've held off on pursuing the goals you have set, leaping right into the big idea may appear impossible and unattainable. You may have tried to make yourself believe in dreams sometime in the past. However, that idea seemed too far off that you could not believe it was possible to achieve it. The struggle to believe it was achievable could be a reason why you believe that it's not feasible instead of providing an illusion that you can achieve whatever you want to achieve. This is, of course, not precisely what you're attempting to accomplish when you dream about your goals as the idea will be expected to inspire your mind, not force you to believe that reaching the dream is impossible.

Instead of jumping headlong into huge goals that cause people to think that it is excessive or unattainable, instead start with a smaller goal. Keep in mind that the grand goal is the ultimate one however, you should be able to dream of small goals, because in the present, which appears to be more realistic and feasible for you now. Let's take an example: you'd like to become the chief executive officer of the organization which you work for yet as of today it is only an employee in one of the lower levels. It is possible that your goal is to be promoted to the next level of management that you're at. Perhaps you have dreams of having a penthouse or an enormous mansion up an incline, but currently you're struggling to make rent payments, and this dream may seem unattainable as well as far away. Instead of creating that as the current goal let yourself imagine a dream that is easier to achieve, for instance can afford to pay a lot of rental costs while putting aside more money. Dreaming in increments in this way means you are able to believe in something that can be reasonable to be a believer about at the moment in your life, and is feasible for you to attain. Once you've achieved this goal, you are able to make the goal higher and higher until you can achieve your ultimate goal that at the moment, appeared to be completely out of your grasp. However, you must keep your dream in the forefront and accessible at all times.

In determining what dream level is realistic for you, there's no correct or incorrect. Some people find that having no money and making an additional $5000 or even $500,000 within the span of a few months appears plausible and achievable, consequently, they get their heads around it and attain it. Others, having nothing and generating additional $500 or $1,000 within a short period is more realistic and feasible which is the one they be convinced of and accomplish. Do not think that you can compare what you consider as reasonable with the things that others believe to be reasonable. it will result in your feeling as if you're playing small. It is important not to be comparing yourself with any other person, but rather to operate with your personal nature and be able to work within your own beliefs about what is believed that is achievable. This isn't a contest however, rather it is a method that allows you to operate with the power of your brain to transform the goals you have set into actual reality.

When you grant yourself the right to imagine, don't feel hesitant to integrate small-scale dreams into your plans as you create your "ultimate" vision, or one that seems too far-fetched or impossible to achieve at the moment. The first thing to remember is that all things are achievable at some moment or the other. Furthermore, the goals that you set for yourself ought to be extremely individual and relevant for you. Regardless of your beliefs about what is feasible today, if you are living a idea that's exciting and important to you, it is definitely worth putting effort and time into. The dream is something you should be thinking about all day long since it makes you feel happy. Think about the moment that you want to see become real, and this can trigger your mind to think of ways to turn it into a realisation.

Every day, make time to think about your dreams. Imagine what you'd like to achieve over the coming days, weeks and months, or about what you'd like to be able to achieve at the at the end each year. Think about where you'd like to be within 2 years, five years, 10, 15 or even in

25 years. Imagine yourself in the future, and consider the things you want to achieve to achieve for yourself. The best way to get started to bring your dream into reality and allow your brain to accept the reality of them is to write about them as well as write them down like they're things you're working towards instead of just dreams you've got. As an example, instead of write, "I dream of one day having enough money to travel the world," you could say, "I am so excited to be working toward my goal of creating enough money to travel the world." Utilizing this kind of language that reflects your desires helps you create positive thoughts in your head which will help you truly believe that the dream you've always wanted is within your reach. This is how you begin to inspire yourself to pursue your goals, no matter how larger ones you consider unlikely to ever be realized.

Believing In Yourself

The most important thing to do in getting off of the couch from a psychological perspective is believing in yourself. One of the most inspiring quotes I've ever encountered that helped me believe in myself was given by Oprah Winfrey. She declared: "You don't become what you want, you become what you believe." The quote itself transformed my outlook in that it helped me understand that having a desire is not enough. It was possible to sit in my couch and wish for a higher salary or better financial situation or a more satisfying relationship an improved lifestyle, and all that I desired, but if this were all I did it would be a long time before I could end up in a state of wanting. If you're simply seeking but not getting the results you want, what's happening inside the person is that they don't believe you're worthy or capable to have what you desire. If you believed in yourself worthy, you'd take actions to get it.

This realization was a big hit in my heart, because in all the books that I read as well as the movies I had observed, I knew I was confident in myself. I was able that I believed in myself and I had the ability to trust myself therefore, surely I should have faith in myself. Wrong. Even though my understanding might have been based on someone who was confident in their own abilities but my life clearly demonstrated my struggle with having faith in my own self. In addition, my life proved to be a lie better than my own brain did. Within my head, my self-confidence was telling me that I believed in me to shield me from the shock of realizing that I wasn't. It was necessary to confront this difficult realization to alter my situation but so would you.

For a better understanding of what's stopping you from having faith that you are a good person, you have take a moment to listen carefully and closely to the thoughts and feelings that are going on inside your head. When you decide to take action, pay attention to the conversation that is going on in your mind and be attentive to the inner dialogue which is going on.

Within your mind it is possible that you are saying things such as "I am able to do this! I'm confident! I'm capable!" but in the inner dialogue, you may be thinking, "Yeah right! What happens if I fail once more? There is no way I can think I can do it. It's a desire but I'm not quite there at the moment." Many people try to suppress the inner dialogue by chanting affirmations and mantras. However, the reality is that this dialogue remains in existence until you are healed. Whatever you do to drown the noise or yelling on the top of it can alter the fact that at the deepest level, you're having a hard time believing that you are a person who believes in yourself.

When you talk about believing that you are a good person and believe in your capabilities or attempt to move involved in something you are passionate about, pay attention to the deeper conversation that is going on inside your head take note of it and record it. Record exactly what that deep dialogue is saying, to help you be able to clearly discern what's happening in your head beneath the many layers of transformation you're trying to bring about within you. The likelihood is that your thoughts are bound cause pain. It did for me with some thoughts made me cry. In a lot of ways, it felt like I was betrayed and resentful of my self just by realizing what I was thinking about myself. Although it was difficult, it was incredibly effective since it helped me identify the areas in which my connection with me was damaged. I could now be able to clearly understand why I had been putting myself in a position of disadvantage and also what was making it so difficult to take actions and bring about an actual change in my lifestyle.

When you've jotted everything down on paper, then you must begin working towards understanding the reasons these self-limiting beliefs came into existence at all. What was the first place you heard or develop these beliefs and for what reason? What purpose did they intend to benefit you over time, and how effective have they proved in their effectiveness? Do you have the desire to finally bring closure your beliefs, to let go of the old beliefs and adopt new ones that will enable you to move forward in your life?

www.ingramcontent.com/pod-product-compliance
Lightning Source LLC
Chambersburg PA
CBHW071447080526
44587CB00014B/2023